**If Not
for Profit,
for What?**

If Not
for Profit,
for What?

A Behavioral Theory
of the Nonprofit Sector
Based on Entrepreneurship

Dennis R. Young
State University of
New York at Stony Brook
and The Program on
Non-Profit Organizations,
Yale University

LexingtonBooks
D.C. Heath and Company
Lexington, Massachusetts
Toronto

Library of Congress Cataloging in Publication Data

Young, Dennis R., 1943-
  If not for profit, for what?

  Includes index.
  1. Corporations, Nonprofit. 2. Organizational
behavior. 3. Entrepreneur. I. Title.
  HD62.6.Y68   1982   302.3′5   82-48482
  ISBN 0-669-06154-9

Copyright © 1983 by D.C. Heath and Company

Published simultaneously in Canada

Printed in the United States of America

International Standard Book Number: 0-669-06154-9

Library of Congress Catalog Card Number: 82-48482

To Seth, Barry, Cheryl, Mark, and Rosalie,
the crew of my own little venture.

Contents

Figures and Tables

Figures

Tables

Foreword

Dennis Young's study of entrepreneurship in nonprofit organizations emerges at a strikingly appropriate moment in the long history of the U.S. voluntary sector. This country has, since its early days, relied heavily on voluntary nonprofit institutions to carry out a wide range of important social and economic tasks—relied on them more heavily, it seems clear, than any other modern society. But in recent years new pressures have been imposed on the nonprofit sector. It faces new and more urgent demands, generated by the high level of social and cultural services that the American people have come to accept—services that have become more difficult to provide in the face of inflationary pressures, reduced or unreliable endowment returns, and, most recently, dramatic governmental retrenchment. For the nonprofit sector, this is a time of great demand and constraint.

As a result, two central questions about the U.S. nonprofit sector have become more salient than ever before. First, what functions should the nonprofit sector take on, expand, reduce, or abandon—in other words, what is an efficient, equitable, and otherwise appropriate division of labor among the nonprofit, governmental, and for-profit sectors of our society? Second, what avenues lead to increased financial and programmatic effectiveness for nonprofit organizations, and how can such effectiveness be measured in the absence of a conventional market or ballot bottom line?

Neither of these issues can successfully be tackled without a better understanding of the incentive systems that work in the nonprofit sector and that distinguish that sector from the worlds of government and commerce. We must know more about the factors that screen individuals—managers, founders, employees, donors, and volunteers—into one of these three sectors, and more about the incentives affecting their behavior once they have been screened. These incentive systems have a great deal to do with the way different types of organizations behave—and therefore with the appropriate division of labor among organizations. They also have a great deal to do with how nonprofit organizations can improve and measure their performance.

For most of Dennis Young's scholarly life, he has studied alternative institutional arrangements for delivering human services and the incentive structures that characterize the organizational alternatives. His books on day care and foster care broke new ground. Accordingly, when Yale launched its Program on Non–Profit Organizations in 1977, one of the very first people to whom we turned as a possible participant was Professor Young. To the great delight of those of us who were designing the research agenda for this new program, Professor Young was interested in exploring one crucial aspect of the incentives picture: the role of entrepreneurs, those managers and founders of nonprofit organizations who succeed in building or giving new life to voluntary organizations as a result of their own imagination, drive and talent. Professor Young was fascinated by the question of what, in a world without conventional profit incentives, distinguishes entrepreneurs from those in the worlds of government and commerce. We usually associate the word *entrepreneur* with the for–profit arena—indeed, it is a reflection of our limited view of the U.S. economic system that when entrepreneurship is mentioned for the first time to most observers, the common reaction is: "How can there be entrepreneurial activity without profit?" or "You mean, I suppose, a study of how nonprofits can save themselves by engaging in commercial enterprise."

This book should open the eyes of those who entertain so narrow an understanding of entrepreneurship. The culmination of Professor Young's imaginative and energetic travail over the past few years, this book makes it clear that the entrepreneurial spirit is remarkably alive in the nonprofit world, and that entrepreneurial activity extends well beyond the production of commercial revenue for nonprofit groups. (His work also required enormous patience, for nothing is harder than corralling a score of exceedingly busy entrepreneurs, not necessarily interested in scholarship, and getting them to sit still long enough to discuss their work and dreams and frustrations.) If Professor Young's painstaking empirical work, reflected in 21 case studies of entrepreneurship, did nothing more than document the existence of this behavior, so widely doubted or underestimated, it would represent a considerable contribution. But Professor Young's work, by casting a new light on the incentives that spawn entrepreneurial activity in all three organizational sectors, also gives us a far better understanding of the behavior of the various organizational species that inhabit our society. As a result, this work advances by a giant step the twin missions mentioned earlier: developing a better understanding of the division of labor among sectors, and promoting effectiveness within the nonprofit world.

Professor Young thus brings us much closer to developing a general theory of the role and performance of the nonprofit sector in the United States. At the same time, he helps us to think about the difficult policy dilemmas that will arise more and more often in the years to come. (These include, for example: Should regulatory and tax measures encourage all organizations in a given industry such as the nursing home, or hospital, or funeral parlor to become nonprofit? Or to become for-profit? Should we more tightly police the behavior of the managers of voluntary organizations? Or should we loosen the restrictions on their pecuniary rewards?) In addition to these insights, Professor Young's work gives us an extra dividend: it helps us to understand the wellsprings of entrepreneurial activity *outside* the nonprofit sector, at a time when there is acute concern about the level of dynamic and innovative activity in U.S. industry.

A brief account of the Yale Program on Non-Profit Organizations indicates how nicely Professor Young's scholarship fits into the program's overall work. The program is an interdisciplinary center for research on the world of nonprofit institutions: their past, present and potential role in our social order, the financing and management problems they face, their impact on the government and business sectors, and their patterns of governance and accountability. Located within Yale's Institution for Social and Policy Studies, the program was launched by Yale's former president, Kingman Brewster, as a way of redressing a long tradition of scholarly neglect of voluntary institutions. Despite the wide variety of social and economic tasks these institutions perform in the United States, our nonprofit sector has been the least studied and the least well understood aspect of our national life.

The Program on Non-Profit Organizations seeks to stimulate academic inquiry and attention, to build a body of data, theory, and analysis about the nonprofit sector, and to generate research that will help resolve major policy and management issues confronting nonprofit organizations. Approximately 150 senior and junior scholars have participated in the program, representing a wide range of disciplines and using many approaches. Approximately 100 articles, working papers, reports and book manuscripts have emerged to date. As this preface is written, the program is entering its second five-year phase of activity, in which it will explore new research territory; consolidate, on the basis of several cross-cutting themes, much of the work of the first five-year phase; and seek new ways to spread the results of this research to a variety of nonscholarly as well as scholarly audiences.

As we look back on the first five-year phase of this program, a paramount source of pride and pleasure is the work of Dennis Young, which we have been privileged to sponsor and which now reaches the general public with this book.

John G. Simon
Chairman, Program on Non-Profit Organizations, Yale University

Preface

The primary purpose of this book is to develop the rudiments of a theory of behavior of nonprofit organizations on which public policies that govern the use of these organizations for public service can be intelligently based. A review of literature on nonprofit organizations is presented to give the reader a sense of the state of existing theory and knowledge about these agencies. The function of entrepreneurship serves as the point of departure for theory development, necessitating considerable review and discussion of this subject. Thus clarification of the entrepreneurial process and its role in the nonprofit sector occupies a major part of this book and is presented as an important ancillary contribution.

Theory development must be based in empirical observation if it is to be relevant to problems of the real world. To a large extent, documentary literature and the author's general experiences fill this need, but the unique formulation of a theory based on the combined areas of entrepreneurship and nonprofit organizations also calls for original fieldwork. That fieldwork is documented by case studies in the child-welfare sector, available separately but referred to in this book as the author's field studies or observed cases. (See "Human Service Enterprise: Case Studies of Entrepreneurship in Child Welfare," Program on Non-Profit Organizations, Institution for Social and Policy Studies, Yale University, 1981.)

As this book moves from review and clarification of the nonprofit sector and entrepreneurship to development of the theory itself, the style of analysis changes as well. The early discussion is basically factual and documentary in character, leaning heavily on published material. As the theoretical framework is laid out (in chapters 5 through 8), the discussion becomes more inferential, assertive, and even speculative, as assumptions are made and hypotheses offered on the motives and mechanisms through which entrepreneurial activity influences the behavior of the nonprofit sector. Although the assumptions and specifications are based on insights derived from observation, the formulation is necessarily judgmental and open to debate. Statements in this part of the book should thus be viewed as informed intuition rather than hard fact, and the theoretical framework as a whole must therefore be regarded as somewhat rough and tentative, welcoming both logical refinement and empirical verification, but, it is hoped, ringing true in its essential thrust.

Once the rudiments of the theory have been discussed, the book turns to a deductive mode of argument. Implications are derived for the performance of public services, assuming the implementation of alternative public-policy measures that affect the use of nonprofit organizations. This analysis is based on the application of logic, but its results still depend on the veracity of the theoretical assumptions.

The basic purpose of the book is served in these last two stages. The theory of nonprofit behavior is set out so that social scientists may use it as a springboard for further conceptual refinement and as the basis for formulating hypotheses for empirical testing. The policy implications are offered so that, pending acceptance of the theoretical framework, the merits of alternative programs can be more insightfully debated.

Acknowledgments

First and foremost, I would like to express my gratitude to the Program on Non-Profit Organizations of Yale University, which sponsored this study. In particular I want to thank John G. Simon, director of that program, for his unwavering encouragement, support, and guidance. I would also like to express my appreciation to Richard R. Nelson, Susan Rose-Ackerman, Estelle James, Burton Weisbrod, and Michelle White for their helpful substantive comments on various drafts; to Henry Hansmann, James Douglas, and Burton Weisbrod, whose own work has helped me to think about nonprofit organizations; and to Helen Kelly for her editorial suggestions. I am also indebted to dozens of real-world social-service entrepreneurs who gave generously of their time and thought.

I am extremely grateful to Lois Pieretti for her skill and dedication in typing seemingly endless drafts of this manuscript, to Gill Innsley, Elizabeth Summers, and Diane Graham and her staff for their typing contributions, to Ella Selmquist and Sandy Nuhn for their skillful assistance with typing and administrative matters, and to Patricia Schlee for her help with final details.

Finally, I wish to thank the Personal Social Services Research Unit, Keynes College, and the Social Policy Board of Studies, at the University of Kent in Canterbury, for providing staff support and an environment conducive for wrapping up the loose ends of this book. I am especially indebted to Bleddyn Davies, director of the Personal Social Services Research Unit, who invited me to Kent and was a gracious host, and to Ken Judge, the assistant director, whose discussions with me were a source of special help.

Some of the ideas developed in this book were first introduced in Dennis R. Young, "Entrepreneurship and the Behavior of Nonprofit Organizations: Elements of a Theory," in *Nonprofit Firms in a Three Sector Economy*, (ed.) Michelle J. White, Committee on Urban Public Economics, The Urban Institute, reproduced here with permission of the publisher.

1

Overview

Although the histories of some nonprofit-sector organizations go back hundreds of years, often predating existing organizations in business and government sectors, the roles and behaviors of nonprofits in the modern world are less well understood than those of organizations in other sectors. In the United States, nonprofits are alternatively viewed as organizational devices to avoid taxation or as panaceas that would rid certain industries of their greedy, self-serving elements, as trusted institutions that preserve cherished cultural and social-welfare traditions or as unfair and wasteful competitors to profit-making enterprise or government-service provision.

Why has the nonprofit sector been such an enigma and a mystery even to well-educated people? One reason is that there is no simple way of associating nonprofit organizations with a clear-cut purpose or with leaders to whom simple labels and motives can be applied. We are all familiar with the profit-seeking businessman in the commercial sector. We think of the ambitious vote-gathering politician in government. These stereotypes help us conceptualize what makes the business and government sectors function. In the nonprofit sector, however, there seems to be no counterpart—no obvious leadership agent that captures the essence of that sector's drive and motivation. Are there such entrepreneurial agents? Suppose that the following headlines appeared in the business section of the *New York Times*:

New Organization Takes Hold amid Decay of the South Bronx

Agency Established to Computerize Management Information for Local Service Industry

Harlem Service Organization Separates from Parent Company

Historic Merger of Two Organizations Results in One of the Largest Firms in the Industry

From Modest Beginnings, Agency Grows into a Thriving Multimillion-Dollar Statewide Organization

Good Business Management, Aggressive Merger Policy Moves Agency from Near Collapse to Industry Leadership

Agency Opens a New Division; Hopes and Fears Expressed over Effects of New Service Mode on Stability of Overall Operations

1

These could easily be typical stories of entrepreneurial activity in the commercial sector. However, these headlines also succinctly summarize instances of enterprising activity in the nonprofit sector of the economy—specifically, a few of the author's fifteen child-welfare-related, nonprofit case studies. The fact that such cases can be described in the same terms used to describe commercial ventures demonstrates that entrepreneurial leadership is not limited to the business sector (or to government) but is characteristic of the nonprofit sector as well.

One purpose of this book is to focus the attention of scholars, managerial practititioners, and social policymakers on this heretofore neglected area of social and economic behavior—entrepreneurship in the nonprofit context, and the different motivations, risks, constraints, and environmental circumstances guiding enterprising behavior in this arena. A more fundamental purpose of this book, however, is to develop a theory of behavior for nonprofit organizations. Such a theory must be built on an understanding of the driving forces behind organizational actions. Clearly, the study of entrepreneurship is an intellectual window on this question. Where are the driving forces more clearly at work than at the leading edge of activity cut by a sector's entrepreneurs? Hence, where else is the motivational basis for activity in a sector more likely to be revealed? For example, in the for-profit sector enterprising behavior is generally believed to be motivated by material gain, with entrepreneurial managers and capitalists exhibiting their motives in response to market opportunities for such gain. What, then, of the nonprofit sector? The nonprofit sector, like others, is composed of many constituent groups that help shape the economic and organizational environment—managers, workers, board members, clients and consumers, donors and philanthropists, and government regulators, for example. As a prime source of insight, however, it is useful to focus on entrepreneurs, their motives, and the influences that affect their decisions and fundamentally shape the activity of the nonprofit sector.

Field studies show strong and diverse motivating factors in the nonprofit arena and entrepreneurs as dynamic as those who work in the profit sector. In this book the author's case studies and other reports of entrepreneurial activity in the literature are used as the basis for classifying these motivations. This book asks, simply: if it isn't profit, what drives enterprising individuals, women and men, to pursue their ventures in the nonprofit context? That starting point is used to build a theoretical framework that extrapolates from entrepreneurial motivations to behavior of organizations and sectors as a whole.

To what end is this theory-building exercise directed? In short, the purpose is to extend scholarly understanding of nonprofits and to contribute to policy discussions concerning the use of these agencies to deliver public services. Certainly, as discussed in the next chapter, there is a growing academic interest in the theory of nonprofit organizations. The nonprofit sector still constitutes a lacuna for scholars, however, particularly for students of microeconomic theory. What are the reasons and justifications for establishing nonprofit organizations, and how can a theory of the firm, analogous to the classical theory of the profit-making firm or the newer economic models of government bureaus be developed for nonprofits? Scholars have only recently begun to seriously address such questions. This book is intended to contribute to this embryonic literature, but in an unconventional way, by constructing a behavioral theory based on the processes of screening, or self-selection, through which entrepreneurs with alternative motivational leanings choose the industries and sectors in which they engage in enterprising activity. The theory developed here views nonprofit organizational behavior not in isolation, but in the context of other sectors that exist alongside it. The thrust of the theory is that entrepreneurs of different motivations and styles sort themselves out by industries and economic sectors in a way that matches the preferences of these entrepreneurs for wealth, power, intellectual or moral purposes, and other goals with the opportunties for achieving these goals in different parts of the economy. Once screened, such entrepreneurial agents are assumed to be largely responsible for giving each sector its particular behavioral flavor and performance characteristics.

Important, substantive differences exist between the screening, or self-selection, model of behavior developed here and the constrained maximization approach of conventional microeconomic theory of the firm. The latter postulates that an agency (nonprofit or otherwise) has some clear objective function that it maximizes, subject to a budget or other resource limitation. We can gain a glimpse of the difference between the two approaches by considering what would happen if additional monies were suddenly granted to nonprofit agencies in a given industry. The conventional theory predicts more of the same type of behavior, that is, achievement of the original objective, but at some higher level of output. The screening framework, however, anticipates more fundamental changes in purpose and direction as shifts occur among sectors in the distribution of entrepreneurial motivations.

In general, an advantage of the multisector framework over narrower and more monolithic approaches to modeling of nonprofits is that it seems more capable of considering the potential effects of changes in ground rules and opportunity structures that alter the position of nonprofits in an industry relative to organizations in other sectors. For example, what happens if nonprofits are favored by government in funding, licensure, or taxation in a particular industry? In essence, the screening theory anticipates that the distribution of entrepreneurial talent will be altered, with consequent implications for the sector's motivational content and, hence, behavior, over time. This kind of difference in thrust between the conventional approach and the approach taken here, with its concommitant implications for both scholarly understanding and practical policy formulation, constitutes the most important contribution of this book.

Many important policy issues hinge on improved understanding of the behavior of nonprofit organizations. For example, various societal forces have conspired in recent years to threaten the viability and independence of nonprofit institutions in higher education, social services, and a number of other areas. Are these institutions worth saving? If so, what are their special virtues and what are the implications of rescuing them with public dollars? Answers to such questions require knowledge of how such agencies perform under alternative opportunities and constraints, compared with institutions from other sectors that might replace them.

In other areas, particularly in the fine arts and museums, where nonprofits hold dominant positions in industries that have traditionally been privately funded in the United States, government has moved toward greater public subsidies, in part to permit expansion and greater citizen appreciation and participation. Should such support be confined to nonprofits? Can the infusion of such resources be expected to change the behavior of these nonprofit organizations? By attracting a wider spectrum of entrepreneurial motivations, the answer may well be yes. Clearly, a fuller understanding of nonprofit behavior would be helpful in the consideration of these matters.

In still other industries, the problems associated with service provision in the governmental or proprietary sectors have prompted policymakers to consider a more significant role for nonprofits in providing services. In certain areas of applied research, for example, nonprofit think tanks have been created as alternatives to use of proprietary consulting firms or in-house government staffs. In large proprietary sectors, such as day care and nursing homes for the elderly, abuses have led to serious proposals to "nonprofitize" these industries. Again, evaluation of these proposals requires some conceptual basis for understanding how such a policy can be expected to affect the behavior of participating nonprofit agencies.

At first, the oil-and-water-like mix of the two subjects—entrepreneurship and nonprofit organizations—may seem strange. Most of us have been acculturated to the notion that entrepreneurship is solely a function of the commercial marketplace. To the contrary, however, entrepreneurship is the key to unlocking some of the doors to better understanding of the world of nonprofit organizations.

This book divides into two parts. Chapters 2 through the first half of chapter 5 describe nonprofit organizations and the entrepreneurship process, establishing the background for the theory developed in the rest of the book. Chapter 2 provides a general discussion of the nonprofit sector, its size and character in the United States and the contributions scholars have made to date toward understanding why it exists and how it behaves.

Chapter 3 develops the concept of entrepreneurship, explaining that contrary to some popular notions, entrepreneurship is not confined to the profit-making sector but accurately denotes mobilizing and catalytic activity in all sectors. The chapter also provides examples of nonprofit entrepreneurial activity in various parts of the service economy. Chapter 4 extends the discussion of entrepreneurship by describing some typical scenarios for venture activity and the economic and social conditions in which they take place. The first part of chapter 5 reviews the literature on motivations that underlie entrepreneurial behavior.

The latter part of chapter 5 begins to establish a theory of nonprofit behavior by specifying stereotypes intended to capture the alternative motivations and styles of entrepreneurs.

Chapters 6 and 7 outline the processes of screening through which alternative entrepreneurial types are sorted into industries and into economic sectors within industries. These chapters identify the structural factors that cause particular varieties of entrepreneurs to select careers, employment, and venture initiatives in certain organizational contexts rather than in others. As such, sectors of a given economic and organizational character can ultimately be associated with particular mixes of motivational and behavioral patterns.

Chapter 8 presents a postscreening perspective by assuming that entrepreneurial populations have been sorted into place and asking how the behavior of (screened) entrepreneurs will be shaped by the constraints of the sectors in which they operate. The discussion explicitly recognizes the relatively loose accountability structures associated with nonprofit organizations, and hence the margin of discretion afforded entrepreneurs. As such, ultimate behavior patterns will reflect both entrepreneurial indulgence in their own motives and adaptation to the rules imposed by the structures in which they operate.

Chapter 9 is a slight but significant digression, which considers the long-term behavioral implications of entrepreneurial activity. Here it is argued that differences in entrepreneurial motivation (resulting from screening) affect organizational behavior not only at the time of venture start-up but also over time. Specifically, the strength of entrepreneurial commitments to particular ventures and host organizations is seen to vary by type of motivation, leading to differences in the long-run success probability as well as the long-run consistency of behavior of the organizations in which entrepreneurs work.

In chapter 10, the theory is brought together and given a normative light by focusing on social-performance criteria and public-policy alternatives. Various entrepreneur-based behavior patterns are considered in terms of four fundamental criteria—trustworthiness, responsiveness, efficiency, and innovation. Subsequently, five major types of public-policy thrusts are considered: (1) the proposal that all agencies in an industry be made nonprofit; (2) the restriction of entry by new organizations into the non-profit sector; (3) the professional licensing of personnel in a given industry; (4) the targeting of public resources to the nonprofit sector of a given industry; and (5) more intensive policing of the regulatory constraints that apply to nonprofit organizations. These kinds of policies are seen to alter the screening and internal accountability mechanisms of sectors in an industry, and hence the behavioral tendencies and social-performance patterns that emerge. Thus the theoretical framework proves to be useful in developing the implications of public-policy initiatives over a range of options.

Overall, the analysis developed in the latter part of this book may be characterized as a descriptive, sector-level theory of behavior. It is sector-level in the sense that it describes in a qualitative way the statistical tendencies and patterns of entrepreneurial populations and groups of organizations in an economic sector, rather than pinpointing specific deterministic objectives and outcomes at the level of individual organizations or people. In particular, the phenomenon of screening by which entrepreneurs are seen to sort themselves into different economic sectors, described in chapters 6 and 7, may be thought of as a random process that allows deviations, mistakes, and changes of mind by individuals and is subject to idiosyncrasies of context, history, and other elements of chance but still provides a roughly accurate picture of outcomes in the sectoral aggregate.

The theory developed here is also essentially descriptive, or positive, in character, in the sense that it models the world as it appears to be rather than as it should be according to some criterion of social justice or efficiency. Rather than trying to directly uncover the logic or justification for having particular industries organized in a certain way, this book asks why, in light of ambient economic and organizational conditions, we tend to observe certain patterns of behavior. However, chapter 10 finally does attempt to draw from this descriptive analysis some normative implications for social performance and public-policy formulation.

A final word about research sources is in order here. Much of the thinking contained in this book derives from my experiences in developing the aforementioned series of twenty-one case studies which focus largely on child care but cover a variety of services, including management-information, consulting, education, and mental-health services. The cases include the founding of new organizations as well as the formation of new programs within existing organizations in the nonprofit, proprietary, and government sectors.

The case studies provide a source of depth, because each one probes intensively into the circumstances and motivations for the venture at issue.

Obviously, however, the relatively small number of cases required that other sources be investigated as well. Thus many references from the literature and the news media, cited throughout the book, have been consulted to enlarge the perspective and to put the insights derived from the cases into broader focus.

2 The Nonprofit Sector

Current interest in the private nonprofit sector of the American economy, by scholars and policymakers, has been stimulated by both the growing significance and the recent struggle of many organizations in this category.[1] The absolute size of the nonprofit sector only hints at its importance. Although sector definitions differ, there is agreement that the private nonprofit sector constitutes about 5 percent of overall economic activity, by various measures. Calculations by Ginsberg (1973) show that private nonprofits account for approximately 8 percent of employment and 5 percent of gross national product (GNP).[2] Tideman (1974), using a more restricted sector definition, estimates employment at 5 percent.[3] According to estimates made by Weisbrod, private nonprofit organizations, in particular, those designated as exempt from corporate taxes by the Internal Revenue Service (IRS), represented 5.2 percent of all corporations, partnerships, and proprietorships in the United States in 1979, received 3.5 percent of all revenue, and held 4.3 percent of the total assets of business firms in 1975–1976.[4] Other estimates of assets are higher.[5]

More important, however, the nonprofit sector is concentrated in such strategic areas as health, education, and social services (welfare), which together in 1976 represented 64 percent of all nonprofit revenue.[6] Nonprofits represent a major proportion of member institutions in such key service sectors as hospitals, residential facilities for the handicapped, disturbed, or dependent, museums, and colleges and universities. Furthermore, in the performing arts, religion, advocacy, and research, private nonprofits constitute significant, if not overwhelming, proportions of industrial activity.

Moreover, as Weisbrod and others have indicated, the nonprofit sector—specifically that part of the sector comprising organizations to which contributions are tax deductible—seems to be growing somewhat faster than the rest of the economy. Whereas the number of profit-making firms (proprietorships, partnerships, and corporations) increased roughly 3.3 percent per year in the early 1970s (1970–1975),[7] the number of nonprofit firms of tax-deductible status increased at a rate of 7.3 percent per year (1971–1976).[8] Similarly, gross receipts of these two sectors exhibited annual rates of increase during the same periods of 15 percent versus 20 percent. Over a longer term, Hirstand reports that nonprofits' expenditures moved from 3 percent of GNP in 1960 to 5 percent in 1973,[9] and Clarkson indicates that the number of private, tax-exempt organizations reported by the IRS more than tripled between 1965 and 1972.[10]

Nonetheless, amid this apparent prosperity there is serious worry about the future of many nonprofit organizations and the viability of the sector as a whole. The concern is especially acute in certain industries. For example, in higher education the Carnegie Council reports that one-quarter of private colleges are in trouble.[11] At a time when rates of failure among commercial business firms are declining[12], financial failures among organizations in a wide variety of areas—higher education, social service, the arts, even hospitals—are commonplace; indeed, proposals to merge and consolidate to preserve existing operations are almost routine. Furthermore, as government has come to finance a large proportion of the services delivered by nonprofit organizations, especially research, health care, social services, higher education, and the arts, serious concerns have arisen over the flexibility and vitality of this once truly independent sector. (See Rose-Ackerman and Nielson for a review of financing patterns.)[13]

If there is any agreement among observers on what is happening to the nonprofit sector, it is that this sector is changing. Agencies are dropping out, consolidation is taking place, finances are shifting, yet the number of new organizations is also growing, apparently faster than in the profit-making sector, and substantial numbers of innovative programs are developing. Charitable contributions are faltering as giving declines as a proportion of GNP,[14] but governmental financing and sales revenues have grown significantly.[15] By Weisbrod's calculation, volunteer labor devoted to nonprofit organizations has outpaced the general growth in the labor force in the 1960s and 1970s.[16]

If scholars are to understand the changing role of the nonprofit sector and the behavior of its member organizations and if policymakers are to deal intelligently with issues concerning the use and regulation of nonprofits for public purposes, then a more precise and robust knowledge base will ultimately be required—not just statistical information but a better conceptual frame of reference than is presently available. First, the nonprofit sector must be broken into its component parts and member organizations classified by their various types and purposes, because this sector seems much too diverse to be understood by a single characterization or model. Second, a theory must be developed for explaining the existence of nonprofits in terms of their special advantages and roles vis-à-vis governmental and profit-making organizations. Third, behavioral models must be synthesized to explain how nonprofit organizations decide on the nature, quantity, quality, costs, and other aspects of their services and operations. Despite the novelty of the study of nonprofits as an academic discipline and the enormity of the subject, scholars have already made important contributions to these classification, theory-building, and modeling tasks.

Classification of nonprofits must begin with a definition. What is a nonprofit organization? The basic answer, offered by Hansmann, is that an organization is nonprofit if it is prohibited by law from distributing surplus revenues (that is, receipts less expenditures, or profits) to individuals (owners).[17] This is the so-called nondistribution constraint, which requires that employees of a nonprofit organization receive reasonable salaries not directly determined by the organization's financial performance and that there be no owners or shareholders who receive dividends. As Hansmann is quick to indicate, nonprofit organizations may generate financial surpluses, but these must be retained or spent on activities consistent with the organization's purposes.

The nondistribution constraint is not very limiting in the kinds of organizations that it encompasses. For example, all organizations classified as exempt from corporate income tax by the IRS fit this definition. In particular, the IRS's Activity Code of Exempt Organizations, which, as Feigenbaum points out, serves a function similar to the Standard Industrial Code (SIC) for the profit-making sector, covers the following major functional categories: religious activities; schools and colleges, including research; cultural, historical, and other educational activities, including museums; other instruction and training activities; health services; business and professional organizations; farming and related activities; mutual organizations, including mutual insurance companies and savings banks and farmers' cooperatives; employee- or membership-benefit organizations, including labor unions and fraternal orders; sports, athletic, recreational, and social activities, such as country clubs; youth activities, such as Boy Scouts; conservation, environmental, and beautification activities; housing activities; inner-city or community activities; civil-rights activities; litigation and legal aid; legislative and political activities; advocacy; and additional categories that encompass counseling and assistance to needy individuals, community chests, cemeteries, emergency relief, and so on.[18] Such a bewildering array of activity in which tax-exempt nonprofits are involved makes classification all the more important. Nor, as Hansmann points out, is the IRS list of tax-exempt organizations a complete catalog of nonprofit activity.[19] Nonprofit laws of incorporation vary considerably by state. In some states with liberal incorporation laws a wide range of activities may take place in nonprofit form; in other states with more restrictive laws nonprofits are confined to more narrowly defined charitable and public purposes.

One way to classify nonprofits is to distinguish tax-exempt agencies to which charitable contributions are deductible from personal income taxes from those to which contributions are not deductible. The latter group consists of mutual-benefit organizations, such as farm bureaus, insurance agencies, unions, trade associations, and clubs that provide services and benefits only to their members. Tax-deductible organizations are assumed to serve a broader purpose, to which the general public may wish to contribute or from which it may receive benefits.

Hansmann takes a somewhat different angle in classifying nonprofits, noting that exemption by federal and state governments is somewhat arbitrary and irregular. He chooses to focus on more fundamental aspects of financing and managerial control.[20] In terms of financing, Hansmann differentiates donative from commercial nonprofits, the former being primarily dependent on charitable contributions for support and the latter depending mostly on revenues from sale of services to individuals or to governments via fee-for-service contracts. On the managerial dimension, Hansmann distinguishes mutual from entrepreneurial nonprofits, the former being controlled by patrons or members through a democratic process and the latter controlled by a self-perpetuating board of directors independent of the membership or clientele. Hansmann's classification is really a two-dimensional spectrum, because many nonprofits exhibit mixtures of contributory and sales financing and membership versus trustee control. Nonetheless, it is a useful classification for differentiating prominent varieties of nonprofit organizations in a rough way. For example, political lobby groups, such as Common Cause or college alumni associations, are mutual-donative nonprofits; country clubs or professional associations, for example, the American Economic Association, could be classified as mutual-commercial nonprofits; charities such as the Salvation Army, the Red Cross, or free museums are donative-entrepreneurial organizations; and hospitals, nursing homes, and research institutes are basically entrepreneurial-commercial in nature. Some nonprofits are harder to classify in terms of Hansmann's four-way scheme. Universities, for example, are financed by both tuition and contributions and are governed by trustees who are often elected from the ranks of alumni (who can be viewed as patrons or members).

There are, of course, many other dimensions along which nonprofit organizations can be differentiated. Nonprofit organizations vary tremendously in size, from those with annual operating budgets of $100,000 or less to those with annual budgets in the tens of millions of dollars. Another differentiating characteristic of nonprofits is the style and culture of an agency—for example, its orientation toward business management and efficiency or toward professional disciplinary interests and research and toward self-determination versus orientation to a larger system or network of agencies.[21] As indicated by Sarason,[22] Lehman,[23] and others, the presence of networking is a significant phenomenon in the nonprofit social and health services. One important facilitator of such a network orientation is the affiliation of organizations with charitable or planning systems, such as The United Fund or health and welfare councils. A particularly important affiliation in some areas—especially in social services, health, and education—is the connection to a religious system, for example, the Catholic Charities or the Federation of Jewish Philanthropies. In a number of the author's case studies membership or lack of membership in a federation is seen to significantly influence organizational behavior.

Within this taxonomic state of understanding of nonprofit organizations it is possible to focus on particular varieties for more intensive study. My concern here is with entrepreneurial, commercially oriented nonprofits, because these are the nonprofit agencies primarily engaged in public-service delivery. Variations in the sources of financing and control will be of special interest. Concentration will also center on "deductible" organizations, which are generally formed with some element of public purpose in order to solicit private donations. Attention is not confined to agencies of a particular size, style, or affiliation, however. My interest is to reflect broadly on the activity of nonprofits in the delivery of general public services in areas such as social welfare, health, education, research, and the arts, where, conceivably, services may be carried out through the public or profit-seeking sectors as well. In this manner, I hope to be able to highlight the process of sector choice as well as the behavioral implications of the nonprofit alternative.

The theory explaining the existence of, or rationale for, nonprofit organizations has various strands. Contributions by Weisbrod and Hansmann are some of the most notable to date. Weisbrod essentially asserts that nonprofit organizations have arisen as a consequence of unsatisfied demands for public goods.[24] This is a kind of government-failure argument, wherein the public sector is seen as unable to satisfy the demands of some groups who desire a greater quality or quantity of some public services. Hence these groups organize on a voluntary basis to satisfy the collective demand neglected by the government. The large group of donative organizations supported by charitable contributions for which there is no direct *quid pro quo* would seem to offer services with a strong public-goods character. Commercial nonprofits of the mutual variety, supported by membership contributions, also appear to provide collective goods for their admittedly limited publics, and those of the entrepreneurial variety are often financed by public fee-for-service funds and hence are agents if not architects of public purpose.

Hansmann comes to his explanation of nonprofits from the opposite direction of market failure,[25] basing his analysis on earlier work of Nelson and Krashinsky in the area of day care for young children.[26] Hansmann argues that nonprofits arise in areas of activity where the consumer is disadvantaged in his ability to discern or evaluate the quality of services. In essence, Hansmann observes that nonprofits are viewed as more trustworthy by the consumer because of the presence of the nondistribution constraint, which reduces the probability that management will make sacrifices in the quality of services to increase financial returns. Thus nonprofits arise

in such areas as nursing homes, child care, hospitals, education, and research either because consumers (children, the sick, and so on) are incom-
petent judges or because the services involved are too complex for the
layman to evaluate.

An alternative way of characterizing the trustworthiness argument is to
view the problem as an asymmetry of information between producers and
consumers.[27] Michelle White uses this perspective to explain why profit-
making, nonprofit, and governmental suppliers are observed to exist simultaneously in a given area of service, such as day care or nursing care.[28] White
argues that consumers, or consumer agents, for example, parents, make
trade-offs between having to spend time monitoring inherently less trustworthy profit-making suppliers and using the less market-responsive (but
more trustworthy) services of nonprofits or governments. Trustworthiness is
seen to increase, and hence monitoring costs to decrease, as one moves from
profit-making to nonprofit to public suppliers, whereas responsiveness to
consumer preferences, that is, provision of desired price-quality combinations, is seen to vary in the reverse direction. Thus the marginal value of a
person's time, that is the time available for personally monitoring service
quality, determines his sectoral selection of suppliers. This value of time can
be expected to vary by income and other variables, hence organizations in
each sector can be presumed to attract different classes of consumers.

There is an interesting closure between the public-goods and trust
rationales for nonprofits, posed recently by Weisbrod.[29] In particular, Weisbrod observes a growing public demand for trustworthy institutions as goods
and services become more technologically complex over time (such as
medical care, energy production, food additives, legal liabilities, and so on).
Hence he speculates that the growth of nonprofits is a response to this
demand.

Since de Tocqueville's time, the vitality of the American democracy and
economy has been seen to lie in the diversity of its economic and political
system, owing in part to the ability of citizens to organize themselves on a
private, voluntary basis. Thus a traditional argument for nonprofit activity is
its character of public-spirited action, independent of government, decentralized and flexible, yet still community-oriented in nature. As explained by
Douglas, the nonprofit sector is able to serve this function because it is free
of the categorical constraint that requires government to provide its services
on a fairly equal basis to all citizens:

> The extent to which the categorical constraint will limit the freedom and
> constrain the flexibility of the public sector will vary . . . somewhat accord-
> ing to the system of government. . . . Yet there must be a limit to the extent
> to which the law can bend . . . if the principle of equality before the law is
> not to be broached. . . . The private non-profit sector has something of the
> same flexibility of the market sector, but . . . can apply its flexibility to

public goods. . . .[T]he government sector has the . . . drawback that it is
unable to allow citizens to opt out and must therefore either perpetrate the
injustice of compelling citizens to contribute to a service of which they
disapprove, or . . . fail to produce a service needed by [some] . . . de-
serving groups.[30]

The rationale of independent and diverse public-oriented provision
certainly appears to underlie the justification for political lobbying organizations, charities, and other activities that Hansmann might classify as mutual
or donative nonprofits. It would also seem to apply to entrepreneurial-
commercial nonprofits in such service-producing activities as child care,
hospitals, museums, and schools, where the presence of nonprofits serves as
a counterweight to potentially more monolithic governmental or profit-
seeking domination and as an independent source of innovation, treatment
methodology, and policy concepts.

Several scholars have postulated positive models of the behavior of
nonprofit organizations. Interestingly there is not a particularly good fit
between the conceptual rationale for nonprofits as providers of public goods
and as fiduciaries for troubled consumers and the stipulated behavioral
propensities postulated in existing economic models. Niskanen, for example, describes the nonprofit organization as a revenue-maximizing entity
from which agency management derives personal utility from power, prestige, monetary benefits, and so on.[31] Tullock provides a parallel model for
charities,[32] and Pauly and Redisch view the nonprofit hospital as a device for
maximizing physicians' incomes.[33] Etzioni and Doty also take special note
of income-increasing tendencies within nonprofits.[34] Feigenbaum, following the managerial-discretion approach of Williamson[35] and Migué and
Bélanger,[36] postulates that nonprofits will, in effect, maximize profits (surpluses of revenues over minimizing costs), which are then used for both
demand stimulation and managerial reward.[37]

James models the nonprofit university as a source of utility for faculty.[38]
In this model, revenues from undergraduate teaching are seen to subsidize
the research and graduate-school activities that the faculty prefer. Alternatively, Newhouse characterizes the hospital as an output-maximizing agent,
subject to physicians' choices of appropriate quality of services.[39] Carlson
follows a similar approach.[40] Clarkson provides a catalog of such economic
models for describing nonprofit and other types of firms.[41]

The chasm that separates the rather noble-purposed explanations of
nonprofit activity from the skeptical, almost cynical assumptions of the
positive-modeling approaches can be bridged by one view of nonprofit
development: nonprofits are formed and authorized in response to particular public needs—the provision of certain public goods and the delivery of
certain services that require a fiduciary relationship with the consumer.
Certain legal requirements are imposed and privileges granted to nonprof-

its, most notably the nondistribution constraint and tax relief, to encourage compliance with the intended purposes. However nonprofit actors (management) ultimately attempt to test these constraints and manipulate them toward selfish ends. In so doing they may be more successful than their more idealistic colleagues in ensuring their own survival. Hence the noble-purposed nonprofit becomes a means to selfish ends.

Such a view is characteristic of the assume-the-worst, homogeneous maximizing school of economic modeling, which has enjoyed success in application to the profit-seeking sector (for example, the assumption that all managers maximize profits) and some success with respect to the public sector, for example, the budget-maximizing models.[42] Recently, however, the more simplistic homogeneous models have been called into question. In the corporate, profit-making sector, for example, it has been recognized that the separation of ownership from managerial control undermines the assumption of profit maximization. Managers often have the opportunity to indulge in individual expense-preference behavior, some of which might be community minded, professionally oriented, or otherwise nonpecuniary in purpose.[43] In the public sector, in the current era of tax-limiting fervor, simplistic assumptions about budget maximizing will have to be reconsidered as bureaucrats and politicians find rewards for cost cutting as well as for program expansion.

In the nonprofit sector, some models have recognized benevolent or nonpecuniary motivations associated with nonprofit activity. Both Weisbrod and Hansmann have considered the differential motives that draw employees and managers to the nonprofit sector. Hansmann postulates two types of managers—those solely interested in pecuniary gain and those also interested in managing institutions of high quality. He shows that the reduced monetary reward offered by nonprofits acts as a signaling device to attract quality-oriented managers and, as a result, nonprofits will produce outputs of higher quality.[44] Weisbrod follows a similar line in his analysis of the employment choices of law-school graduates.[45] Differentiating between those graduates primarily interested in money and those interested in public-interest legal work, Weisbrod finds that graduates who join public-interest firms accept significant pay reductions relative to graduates with equivalent credentials who work for profit-making law firms.

The works of Hansmann and Weisbrod in the nonprofit sector and work by Tullock[46] and others (Daly)[47] in the public sector emphasize the process of screening in the labor market as the salient mechanism through which different sectors of the economy acquire their motivational characters. Screening or self-selection occurs on the basis of differences in structural variables among sectors (supply-side aspects, as Daly calls them), such as income potential and intrinsic character of the work to be performed. The differential filtering of motivation into sectors that allow room for managerial discretion determines the ultimate behavior of firms. Thus, for nonprofits, according to Hansmann's and Weisbrod's analyses, the screening process may be expected to produce organizational activity that is less tuned to pecuniary aggrandizement than that of firms in the profit-making part of the economy.

Because of the nonprofit sector's size and diversity, full clarification of the behaviors of nonprofit organizations will require extensive work by researchers. The screening approach articulated by Hansmann and Weisbrod, particularly if coupled with empirical investigation, seems likely to be one of the more fruitful strategies for several reasons. First, this approach recognizes that the nonprofit sector exists not in isolation, but in conjunction with other sectors, in most fields of activity. Second, the screening approach acknowledges seemingly obvious differences in motivations among participants within any given field of economic or social endeavor and the common existence of maneuvering room to indulge these motivations. Third, the screening approach postulates that differences in the character of nonprofits versus other forms may appeal to people with certain motivations more than to others. Thus the structural characteristics and opportunities for managerial discretion offered by nonprofits interact with the pool of motivations of potential participants to produce behaviors that distinguish this sector from others. Furthermore, such results may be expected to vary by field or industry, as the motivations of potential entrants and the structural characteristics also vary among industries.

In this book, the idea of screening is used to help explain the differential behavior of organizations in the nonprofit sector by focusing on a particular class of participants—the *entrepreneurs* who mobilize people and resources required to establish new organizations or implement major new programs or policies. In this way I intend to illuminate the reasons that economic activity takes place and that particular types of entrepreneurs participate in the nonprofit sector, and to discern the behavioral tendencies of nonprofits that derive from this selection process. That effort begins with a discussion of entrepreneurship in the next chapter.

Notes

1. Waldemar A. Nielson, *The Endangered Sector* (New York: Columbia University Press, 1979).

2. Eli Ginsberg, "The Pluralistic Economy of the U.S.," *Scientific American*, December 1976.

3. Nicolaus Tideman, *Employment and Earnings in the Nonprofit Charitable Sector*, Commission on Private Philanthropy and Public Needs Compendium of Research, Washington, D.C. (1974).

4. Burton Weisbrod, "Growth of the Nonprofit Sector: Implications for Public Employment and Public Finance" (Paper presented to the Thirty-sixth Congress, International Institute of Public Finance, Jerusalem, August 1980).

5. Henry B. Hansmann, "The Role of Non-Profit Enterprise," *Yale Law Journal*, April 1980. Also, Nielson, *Endangered Sector*.

6. Burton Weisbrod, unpublished calculations based on sample Form 990 tax returns.

7. *Statistical Abstract of the United States, 1978*, U.S. Department of Commerce, Bureau of the Census, p. 561.

8. Weisbrod, "Nonprofit Sector."

9. Lohr E. Miller, "A Quantitative Guide to the Non-Profit Sector of the U.S. Economy" (Draft, Program on Nonprofit Organizations, Yale University, March 1980).

10. Kenneth W. Clarkson and Donald L. Martin, eds., "Introduction," *The Economics of Nonproprietary Organizations* (Greenwich, Connecticut: Jai Press, 1980).

11. Nielson, *Endangered Sector*.

12. *Statistical Abstract*, p. 561.

13. Susan Rose-Ackerman, "Government Grants and Philanthropy" (Draft, Institution for Social and Policy Studies, Yale University, August 1979). Also, Nielson, *Endangered Sector*.

14. Nielson, *Endangered Sector*.

15. *Statistical Abstract*. Also, *Giving in America*, Report of the Commission on Private Philanthropy and Public Needs, Washington, D.C. (1975).

16. Burton Weisbrod, "Economics of Institutional Choice" (Draft, University of Wisconsin, October 1979).

17. Henry Hansmann, "Rationalizing the Basic Legal Framework for Non-Profit Enterprise" (Draft, Institution for Social and Policy Studies, Yale University, September 1979).

18. Susan Feigenbaum, "Some Inter-Industry Relationships in the Nonprofit Sector: Theory and Empirical Testing" (Department of Economics, Claremont Men's College, October 1979).

19. Hansmann, "Basic Legal Framework."

20. Hansmann, "Nonprofit Enterprise."

21. Dennis R. Young and Stephen Finch, *Foster Care and Nonprofit Organizations* (Lexington, Mass.: Lexington Books, D.C. Heath and Company, 1977).

22. Seymour B. Sarason, Charles F. Carroll, Kenneth Maton, Saul Cohen, and Elizabeth Lorentz, *Human Services and Resource Networks* (San Francisco: Jossey-Bass, 1977).

23. Edward W. Lehman, *Coordinating Health Care* (Beverly Hills: Sage Publications, 1975).

24. Burton A. Weisbrod, *The Voluntary Nonprofit Sector* (Lexington, Mass.: Lexington Books, D.C. Heath and Company, 1977).

25. Hansmann, "Nonprofit Enterprise."

26. Richard R. Nelson and Michael Krashinsky, "Two Major Issues of Public Policy: Public Subsidy and Organization of Supply," in *Public Policy for Day Care of Young Children*, eds. Dennis R. Young and Richard R. Nelson (Lexington, Mass.: Lexington Books, D.C. Heath and Company, 1973).

27. Burton A. Weisbrod, "Institutional Choice."

28. Michelle J. White, "On the Optimal Distribution of Activity in a Three Sector Economy" (Draft, New York University, October 1979).

29. Weisbrod, "Institutional Choice."

30. James Douglas, "Towards a Rationale for Private Non-Profit Organizations" (PONPO working paper 7, Institution for Social and Policy Studies, Yale University, April 1980).

31. William Niskanen, *Bureaucracy and Representative Government* (Chicago: Aldine-Atherton, 1971).

32. Gordon Tullock, "Information Without Profit," *Papers on Non-Market Decision Making & Public Choice*, 9 Fall (1966).

33. Mark Pauly and Michael Redisch, "The Not-For-Profit Hospital as a Physicians' Cooperative," *American Economic Review*, 63 March 1973.

34. Amitai Etzioni and Pamela Doty, *Profit in Not-For-Profit Institutions* (Working Paper, New York: Center for Policy Research, January 1976).

35. Oliver Williamson, *The Economics of Discretionary Behavior*, (Chicago: Markham, 1967).

36. Jean-Luc Migué and Gerard Bélanger, "Toward a General Theory of Managerial Discretion," *Public Choice* 17 (Spring 1974).

37. Feigenbaum, "Inter-Industry Relationships."

38. Estelle James, "A Contribution to the Theory of the Non-Profit Organization" (Draft, State University of New York at Stony Brook, 1978).

39. Joseph Newhouse, "Toward a Theory of Non-Profit Institutions: An Economic Model of a Hospital," *American Economic Review*, 60 March 1970.

40. Robert Carlson, James Robinson, and J. Michael Ryan, "An Optimization Model of a Nonprofit Agency," *Western Economic Journal* (1971).

41. Kenneth W. Clarkson, "Managerial Behavior in Non-proprietary Organizations," in *Nonproprietary Organizations*, eds. Clarkson and Martin.

42. Niskanen, *Representative Government*.

43. Williamson, *Discretionary Behavior*. Migué and Bélanger, "Managerial Discretion."

44. Hansmann, "Nonprofit Enterprise," appendix.

45. Weisbrod, "Institutional Choice."

46. Gordon Tullock, *The Politics of Bureaucracy*, (Washington, D.C.: Public Affairs Press, 1965).

47. George Daly, "Politics as a Filter," *Public Choice* 24 (1981).

3 Entrepreneurship

With few exceptions modern economists have paid scant attention in their conceptual work to entrepreneurship.[1] Conventional microeconomic theory is static, monolithic, and strictly structural in nature, concerned with the interaction of aggregate demand and supply functions (based on simple stereotypes of consumers and firms) and providing minimal insight into the range and variety of behavior of individual consumers or producers. In this same style, the theory views the interaction of supply and demand as an impersonal, automatic equilibrating process and is not concerned with the individuals and dynamic processes through which demanders and suppliers are brought together into new and changing markets. This structural bias of theory—particularly the inattention to market-making behavior—precludes most economists from seriously studying entrepreneurship and leaves the concept of entrepreneurship somewhat ambiguous and unclear.

In everyday usage the term *entrepreneurship* is associated with the organizing and managing of risky economic ventures for profit.[2] Scholars who have wrestled with the concept differ with this definition, and with each other, in terms of its emphasis on risk and profit, its lack of focus on innovation, and its failure to distinguish the entrepreneurial function from that of the manager, the capitalist or financeer, or the inventor. As Hoselitz indicates: "A study of economists' opinions on entrepreneurship leads to strange and sometimes contradictory results. Some writers have identified entrepreneurship with the function of uncertainty-bearing, others with the coordination of productive resources, others with the introduction of innovations, and still others with the provision of capital."[3]

Two questions arise concerning the definition of *entrepreneurship*. First, on what basis can this term be used in non-profit-making parts of the economy? (Clearly this practice is at odds with common usage.) Second, what specifically does entrepreneurship comprise? A precise idea of what is involved in entrepreneurship is needed in order to analyze its implications. Joseph Schumpeter, in his analysis of economic development, gives the classic definition of *entrepreneur*.[4] Schumpeter defines the entrepreneur as the individual who implements "new combinations of means of production." There are five possible types of these new combinations: (1) the introduction of a new economic good; (2) the introduction of a new method of production; (3) the opening of a new market; (4) the conquest of a new source of raw materials of half-manufactured goods; and (5) the carrying out of the new organization of an industry, such as the creation or breaking up of a monopoly.

Schumpeter clearly focuses on implementation of change and innovation, as do other writers. For example, Angel, who studied development of the sun-belt cities of the United States, calls entrepreneurs "innovative capitalists."[5] Matthew Josephson, who wrote on nineteenth-century industrial development, defines the entrepreneur as "one who feels the turn of the current before others."[6] Collins and Moore, who studied individuals who undertook new business enterprises, define entrepreneurship as "the catalytic agent in society which sets into motion new enterprises, new combinations of production and exchange."[7]

Although the focus on innovation narrows the definition of entrepreneur from the broader concept of manager ascribed to by Marshall, the role of innovation in entrepreneurship can be overemphasized.[8] As Schumpeter indicates, *entrepreneur* is not synonomous with *inventor* or *idea generator*, for new ideas must be implemented to effect new combinations. Nor is the focus on innovation restricted to originality. Although Angel asserts that entrepreneurs differ from nonentrepreneurs because the latter "seek only to accumulate capital by mimicking established business methods. . ."[9], Schumpeter's definition would include mimicking behavior if it took place in a new context, for example, existing services to a new consumer group.

Entrepreneurship is usually associated with risk taking. As noted by Collins and Moore, "In the popular conception . . . the independent entrepreneur is a risk-taker—a man who braves uncertainty, who strikes out on his own, and who—through native wit, devotion to duty, and singleness of purpose—somehow creates business and industrial activity where none existed before."[10] Schumpeter's definition, however, quite purposefully contains no explicit reference to risk. Schumpeter's point is to separate the role of entrepreneur from that of capitalist and to indicate that entrepreneurs may undertake no special financial risk in developing new enterprise, as it is others' capital that they are employing:

> The entrepreneur is never the risk bearer. . . .The one who gives credit comes to grief if the undertaking fails. For although any property possessed by the entrepreneur may be liable, yet such possession of wealth is not essential, even though advantageous. But even if the entrepreneur finances himself out of former profits, or if he contributes the means of production belonging to his . . . business, the risk falls on him as capitalist or as possessor of goods, not as entrepreneur. Risk-taking is in no case an element of the entrepreneurial function. Even though he may risk his reputation, the direct economic responsibility of failure never falls on him.[11]

Although financial risk bearing can thus be conceptually separated from entrepreneurship, it is clear why risk is correlated with this function. First, entrepreneurs do often invest their own capital and, indeed, may be required to, in order to give other investors confidence in their commitment. (This situation does not, however, exist in the government and nonprofit sectors or in the context of entrepreneurship by large corporations, where entrepreneurs need not assume fiscal liabilities.) Also, as acknowledged by Schumpeter, risk may be other than financial. The outcomes of entrepreneurial activity are inherently less predictable than other forms of employment, yet entrepreneurs often put their reputations and careers on the line, in public view, with such ventures. Entrepreneuring may be safer than race-car driving, but it is more risky than the typical white-collar job. Furthermore, the inclination to take personal risks helps determine the boldness and innovativeness of ventures undertaken, for there seems an inevitable association between the degree of proposed change and the probability of failure.

Perhaps of the greatest interest here is the apparent connection of entrepreneurship to profit making. Cole, for example, defines entrepreneurship as "The purposeful activity . . . of an individual or group of associated individuals, undertaken to initiate, maintain, or aggrandize a *profit-oriented business* unit for the production or distribution of economic goods and services."[12] Despite the specific reference to the profit-making sector in this and other definitions and the specifically market-oriented context in which Schumpeter's discussion is posed, entrepreneurship is described basically as an organizing and promoting activity, which may be paid for by wages or other means, and which can, indeed must, takes place in all economic sectors—profit oriented or not. Schumpeter's concept of implementing new combinations seems entirely applicable to the production of government, or nonprofit-sector services, although the motives and the specific forms and procedures for undertaking new ventures may differ.

Schumpeter's five types of entrepreneurial venture are based on an industry as the unit of analysis and involve changes in an industry's product, input, consumers, technology, or organizational structure. Entrepreneurs, however, operate not at the industry level, but at the level of the firm—the two levels being synonomous only in the case of a monopoly. From the viewpoint of the entrepreneur, then, it is desirable to classify ventures differently. Although they may be aware of this potential, entrepreneurs do not necessarily seek to change an industry; rather, they aim to implement a successful, firm-level enterprise, if only because the factors under their control, except in the case of a monopoly, operate at the level of the firm.

Collins and Moore describe a basic dichotomy in the form of entrepreneurial ventures—the distinction between setting up new organizations and developing ventures within the context of existing organizations.[13] These authors indicate that the motives of entrepreneurs and the implications of either choice may be quite different. This point will be elaborated later. For the present discussion the relevant consideration is whether the establishment of a new organization or a new program within an existing organization necessarily constitutes an instance of entrepreneurship. The answer depends on whether something new is being done and whether the firm-level action has industry-wide implications of the kind outlined by Schumpeter.

In the case of a new firm or organization, entrepreneurship almost always seems to be involved. New organizations are formed either to fill some empty niche in the industrial landscape—to offer a new product or serve a different set of consumers—or to substitute an improvement in the current regime—for example, use of a new techology, more economical input factors, or change of product quality. Furthermore, the introduction of new organizations inevitably alters the structure of the industry (Schumpeter's fifth criterion), if only slightly. Even where a new organization simply imitates the methods and services of another, some degree of innovation is likely to be involved, except perhaps in establishing franchise outlets, such as fast-food restaurants and automobile dealers.

The class of ventures that take place in the context of existing organizations requires closer inspection. In particular, what constitutes a new enterprise or program within a given corporate structure? Certainly a shift of personnel or the rearrangement or relabeling of boxes on an organization chart should not qualify as an entrepreneurial venture unless it signals a more fundamental change. Various types of changes do qualify, however, in the sense of leading to potentially substantive changes in the industry. Certain of these programmatic changes are obvious. If an organization adopts a new technology, provides a new service, or seeks a new consumer group, it is implementing a new combination and hence entrepreneuring. If an organization undertakes a major expansion (through internal growth or mergers) or diversification of its goods and services, even if these products are conventional, implications may abound for other firms and for the structure of the industry as a whole (for example, a shift from many small to a few large firms). Hence the venture would qualify as entrepreneurial.

Suppose that an organization radically shifts its services from one type to another. If the new service is novel in some sense, then the venture is clearly entrepreneurial, but even if the shift is from one conventional service to another, the venture may be indicative of change in the sense of an industry-wide shift from one source of demand, which is drying up (such as the demand for slide rules), to another, which is growing (for example, electronic calculators).

Another form of programmatic change that takes place in the context of existing organizations and that often indicates entrepreneurial activity is the revival of a failing organization. Organizations begin to fail for a variety of internal and environmental reasons. According to Hirschman's analysis of the processes of "exit and voice" a certain level of oscillation of organizational deterioration and recuperation is to be expected.[14] Correction of routine problems or reduction of slack through enforcement of existing methods and procedures or the shifting of personnel does not constitute entrepreneurship. Often, however, organizational failures are endemic to an industry. As noted above, the demand for certain products or services may decline because of changes in tastes or technological developments; changes in government policies may affect industrial fortunes (witness the role of public-university systems in the decline of some private universities or the effect on railroads of government spending on highways); or industries may age, and their technologies, capital facilities, and personnel capabilities may become obsolete (for example, the domestic steel industry or the older industrial cities of the Northeast). In such cases, entrepreneurial initiatives may succeed in turning organizations around through technological renovations, product reorientation, or structural changes in corporate financing and decision making, and these turnarounds may signal basic changes at the industry level.

In short, several types of developments at the organization (firm) level are strong manifestations of entrepreneurial activity. The establishment of new organizations constitutes one class. The development of new programs in the context of existing organizations is another. Both types of development can include the introduction of new goods or services, service to new consumer groups, introduction of new technical methods or inputs, or innovations in corporate structure and financing. New programs within established organizations may also encompass major growth and expansion or product diversification or simplification. Finally, the turnaround of failing organizations may be indicative of changes in products, clientele, methods, inputs, or financial and organizational strategies, all indicative of entrepreneurship.

In all these cases, of course, entrepreneurship is a matter of degree. New organizations and major programmatic changes in existing organizations (including organizational turnarounds) together provide many interesting cases. In some instances, ventures will be observed at the leading edge of industry-wide change. In other cases, imitative or following behavior may be an equally accurate characterization. In all cases, there will be some originality and some imitation, some industry-wide implications and some implications peculiar to the individual firm. It becomes a matter of judgment as to what constitutes a legitimate case of entrepreneurship and what does not. Nonetheless, the qualitative character of entrepreneurship is clear, as is the notion that new organizations and internal programmatic developments of the kinds just discussed are relevant manifestations.

The inclusion of new organizations and internal programmatic developments helps make obvious the omnipresence of entrepreneurship across the various sectors of the economy. Although the incidence and distribution of these events differ among the public, nonprofit, and profit-making sectors, both new organizations and new program developments occur continually in all sectors. New governments occasionally form to replace old ones or to fill in new niches (metropolitan governments in some urban areas, new special districts or municipal incorporations, and so on). New government bureaus are formed with greater frequency, and program and policy changes are even more common. Failing governments also manage to extricate themselves from difficulty through major structural and programmatic shifts. Hundreds of nonprofit agencies are newly incorporated annually, and many new programs are established by the thousands of existing nonprofit organizations, associations, and federations. And struggling nonprofit universities, social-service agencies, fine-arts, and performing-arts organizations, and the like often save themselves from financial failure through entrepreneurial initiative.

Such a litany is, of course, familiar for the profit-making sector, in which many new businesses start each year, new products and technologies are developed, major corporations undertake multiple initiatives internally, and many firms come back from the edge of bankruptcy.

Because this book is fundamentally concerned with the nonprofit sector, particular illustrations from that part of the economy are useful to provide a specific sense of the nature and variety of nonprofit entrepreneurship and to indicate that nonprofit entrepreneurship is indeed a real, significant, and widespread phenomenon. This aim is most easily accomplished by reviewing a few fields of endeavor in which nonprofit activity is common.

The author's field studies in the broad field of child welfare focus on various manifestations of entrepreneurial venture. Several cases illustrate the founding of new nonprofits from scratch, and other cases describe new agencies that are spin-offs of parent organizations. One study reviews the formation of a new agency through the merger of two parent agencies. Another documents the experience of a social agency that radically changed its services (to juveniles) from one type (detention) to another (diagnostic). Still other cases illustrate the creation of new services by established agencies. A final set of studies describe dramatic turnarounds and growth of previously failing organizations.

Additional documentation of nonprofit entrepreneurial ventures in social services exists in the literature. For example, a collection of vignettes of over one hundred successful self-help projects in economically disadvantaged communities across the United States is presented in *Uplift*, under the auspices of the U.S. Jaycees Foundation.[15] The projects cover a number of functional areas, including local economic development, education, employment opportunity, housing, social services, health services, offender rehabilitation, and community organization. The vignettes report the efforts of local people—housewives, working people, clergy, handicapped people,

social workers, minority-group leaders, exoffenders, reformed alcoholics—
to organize new programs and establish nonprofit organizations dedicated
to solving or servicing some of the problems in their local communities.

Other literature is more confined and focused on particular cases. In a
study of foster-care agencies by Young and Finch, several cases of entrepreneurial activity are cited, including an agency that was converted from
proprietary to nonprofit form, agencies that changed or grew rapidly over
short periods of time, agencies that developed innovative programs for
delinquent children, and newly established agencies.[16]

Other children's service ventures have received more notoriety. Rever-
end Bruce Ritter has often been cited for his path-breaking developments at
Covenant House, a nonprofit child-care agency—notably for its Under 21
program, which services teenagers in the Times Square area of New York
City who have run away from home and become involved in prostitution and
pornography.[17] Other examples include Hope for Youth, a group home for
abandoned or abused boys, established on Long Island in 1969 by Elizabeth
Golding, a retired family court judge;[18] the Human Resources Center, an
education and training institution for the physically handicapped, founded
in 1953 by Henry Viscardi, himself crippled from birth;[19] and a home for boys
in Guatemala, established in 1977 by John Wetterer, an American Vietnam
veteran, with the support of the American Friends of Children, which he
also founded.[20] Finally, a case of youth-oriented social-service entrepreneurship is described in detail by Goldenberg in *Build Me a Mountain*, which
documents the formation and early operation of the Residential Youth
Center in New Haven, Connecticut.[21] The venture, which entails entrepreneurship by Goldenberg and a few of his associates, was funded by the
U.S. Department of Labor through New Haven's community action agency
and administered in conjunction with the Psycho-Educational Clinic of Yale
University.

Another interesting case, provided by Moore and Ziering, describes
several entrepreneurial efforts to address the heroin-addiction problem in
New York City in the mid 1960s.[22] Moore cites new programs organized
within the city's Addiction Services Administration and Health and Hospitals Corporation as well as a venture based at the nonprofit Beth Israel
Hospital. The latter was led by Vincent Dole, who developed the technique
of methadone maintenance and organized and expanded a program within
Beth Israel with public-sector (city) support.

The particular area of services to the elderly has witnessed a burgeoning
of entrepreneurial activity over the last two decades. In the context of
residential care, most of the action has been proprietary, but nonprofit
activity also abounds.[23] Recent case studies of newly established nursing
homes by Grennon and Barsky provide detailed examples of two nonprofit
nursing-home ventures.[24] Other examples are referenced by Vladeck.[25]

Nonresidential services to the elderly are dominated more heavily by non-profits. Fueled in part by provisions of the Older Americans Act, initiatives in this field have skyrocketed. Activities include congregate meeting facilities, food and homemaker programs, transportation, health, and a variety of other services designed to enable the elderly to live in the community rather than in nursing homes. An outstanding example of nonprofit entrepreneurial activity in this area is the Minneapolis Age and Opportunity Center, Inc. (MAO), organized by Daphne Krause in 1969.[26] The MAO is considered a pioneering venture, developed from scratch by a highly energetic and determined layperson, to provide a range of health, home-support, economic, and other assistance to elderly in need in the Minneapolis region.

The growth of emergency-relief organizations and other major charities is a prime manifestation of nonprofit entrepreneurship and is often in the public eye. Some international efforts, such as Oxfam, established in England almost forty years ago to provide relief from famine,[27] or the now-legendary work of Nobel laureate Mother Theresa of India,[28] which has included the establishment of some 158 branch houses in thirty-one countries, are examples. In the United States, organizations like the Red Cross and the Salvation Army have long histories of organizing emergency-relief programs of various kinds.

The fund-raising activity of emergency-relief and other types of charities—specialized, like the American Cancer Society, or generalized, such as the United Way—constitute a rather visible aspect of nonprofit entrepreneurship. Fund raising for charitable causes has come to represent a business in many minds, raising suspicions about the wisdom and efficiency, if not propriety, with which such funds are disbursed. Certainly, as noted by Rose-Ackerman and others, the behavior of United Funds in establishing payroll-deduction plans and consolidating the fund-raising functions of multiple charitable causes through unified fund drives represents entrepreneurship—a developing of new combinations for production, in Schumpeter's terms.[29] (It has also engendered some resistance and indignation, as many such ventures do.)[30]

United Way and other large charities are nonsectarian, but similar entrepreneurial behavior is found in the church-oriented charities as well. Merging of the fund-raising efforts of such organizations as the United Jewish Appeal and the Federation of Jewish Philanthropies in New York is one example. Fund raising is not the only direct aspect of entrepreneurship manifested by church-sponsored and other charities, however. Aside from funding various established non-profit operating agencies, such charities become involved in setting up new corporations and administering direct-service programs in a variety of fields. For example, Catholic Charities of New York has been active in promoting local parishes to establish senior-citizen centers and in establishing certain innovative programs, such as hospices for the terminally ill.

Another interesting entrepreneurial tack taken by some charities, especially those which have funded causes addressed to problems that have ultimately been remedied or ameliorated, is diversification into new fields. The branching of the March of Dimes from polio research into the problem of birth defects and of charities for the blind into services for the multiply handicapped provide familiar examples. Still, new charities continue to be formed, often reflecting the personal concerns of founders. An example is the Committee to Combat Huntington's Disease, established by the widow of Woody Guthrie, the folksinger who died of that illness.[31]

Another entrepreneurial direction taken by some charities and churches is providing services through commercial-type ventures. For example, the Agency for the Blind as well as a number of churches have been directly involved in housing construction for the elderly and handicapped.[32] Fund raising through commercial-type activities—cake sales, benefit performances, raffles, auctions—has become an established practice for churches and other charities and is not confined to this part of the nonprofit sector. Many nonprofit organizations in a variety of fields have come to rely on commercial activities peripheral to their main purpose, such as sale of publications, property rental, gift shops, and insurance and travel programs, to generate revenues in support of service programs. Where such activity competes with private business, such nonprofit entrepreneurship has generated resentment and required scrutiny by the IRS.

Philanthropic foundations—large ones, such as Rockefeller, Mellon, Ford, and Carnegie, established through amassed family fortunes; those such as Johnson, Exxon, and Lilly, founded by large corporations; and many smaller ones—are an integral part of the world of nonprofit entrepreneurship. Foundations differ from charities—they have to give away money rather than collect it. In terms of entrepreneurial activity, however, there are similiarities. For example, there are efforts, such as the New York Community Trust, to consolidate small, individual foundation resources to permit the funding of larger and more meaningful projects and to allocate resources in a more systematic way. More important, in providing services foundations have been active in the design and support of new ventures over a wide spectrum of social causes and often become involved in individual projects and programs. Areas such as research, higher education, social and economic development, and health are replete with illustrations of integral foundation involvement. The 1972 study by Nielsen reviews a variety of such examples;[33] in his subsequent book, Neilsen cites Andrew Carnegie and John D. Rockefeller as the developers of the modern foundation as a vehicle of social change and credits the Ford Foundation with stimulating modern-day support for the arts.[34]

The field of higher education has produced several examples of nonprofit entrepreneurship since World War II. *Academic Transformation*, edited by Riesman and Stadtman, focuses on the crises of the 1960s and discusses such examples as the innovations of Antioch, changes in programs at the University of Pennsylvania and Princeton, and the growth of Stanford.[35] The latter is by now a legendary success story, documented recently in the alumni paper, encompassing the transformation of a scholastically limited and financially insecure university into one of the economically and educationally strongest in the country.[36] President Wallace Sterling, Provost Frederick Terman, and others are credited with such major coups as the development of the Stanford Industrial Park and Stanford Medical Center, which exploited the riches of the university's real estate and emerging new technologies to push Stanford to the forefront of technical and academic excellence.

More recently, the resurgence of New York University (NYU) parallels the Stanford experience somewhat in its revival aspects. Under the leadership of John Sawhill, and with a boost from sales of (and reinvestment of revenues from) certain key assets, NYU expanded and began new construction at a time (the 1970s) when higher education was generally perceived to be in difficult straits.[37] Latent assets (Stanford's land, NYU's ownership of the C.F. Mueller spaghetti company) help explain these successes, but such assets by no means ensured active engagement in entrepreneurship. An interesting case to watch will be Emory University, recently the recipient of $100 million from Robert W. Woodruff of Coca-Cola.[38]

A rather offbeat example of entrepreneurship in higher education is provided by Nova University in Florida, which has pioneered in such areas as computer-assisted instruction and off-campus programs.[39] Nova was saved from bankruptcy in 1970 by the New York Institute of Technology, whose president, Alexander Schure, became chancellor of Nova. The expansionism of the New York Institute of Technology and the maverick nature of Nova's programs have stirred some local resentment in Florida, particularly since Nova became the prospective recipient of certain charitable bequests. Schure, however, appears to have a keen idea of what his own entrepreneurship is all about, arguing that institutions need to identify and exploit marketing trends to survive.

As chapter 4 will show, entrepreneurship commonly arises from institutional adversity. Stanford, NYU, and Nova bear witness to this. Other cases include the absorption of the troubled Peabody College by Vanderbilt[40] and the takeover of Simon's Rock College by Bard College.[41] Another manifestation is the burgeoning of extension programs and the opening of out-of-state branches by many universities, in a "frantic search for students"[42] Even in the era of fiscal stringency and projected enrollment declines, adversity is not the only springboard for entrepreneurship in higher education. Tufts, for example, has opened a major veterinary school in anticipation of synergistic growth with other health-science units on the campus.[43] Professional education has witnessed a great deal of recent nonprofit entrepreneurship, not only in the expansion of schools in such growing disciplines as law, medicine, and business, but also in the birth of a whole generation of interdisciplinary schools since the late 1960s, for example, the School of Organization and Management at Yale, the Kennedy School of Government at Harvard, and the School of Urban and Public Affairs at Carnegie-Mellon University. In a related development, universities and their faculties have seized on the opportunities for funded research by establishing a myriad of nonprofit research institutes, such as Stanford Research Institute, Yale's Institution for Social and Policy Studies, Columbia's Center for Policy Research, and Michigan's Institute for Social Research.[44]

Research institutes outside the university context are another prime manifestation of recent nonprofit entrepreneurship. Such organizations as the Urban Institute (under the leadership of William Gorham), the Vera Institute of Justice, and the Research Triangle Institute have emerged as major providers of research and policy studies in the 1960s and 1970s, while older institutes such as the Brookings Institution and RAND Corporation have grown and diversified significantly in this area.[45]

As reviewed by Nielsen, health care is another field in which nonprofit entrepreneurship has flourished in various forms.[46] Recently, organizational units centered on medical innovations—open-heart-surgery units, organ-transplant programs, and burn-treatment centers—have been started in nonprofit medical centers. An especially interesting development is the hospice conceived by Dame Cicely Saunders in England and recently implemented in a number of U.S. nonprofit settings, including the Good Samaritan Hospital in West Islip, New York and Mercy Hospital in Rockville Center, New York.[47] These hospices are designed to provide a comfortable, hospitable environment for the terminally ill.

The rising costs, increasing governmental support, and growing sophistication and specialization of health care have spurred a number of different types of nonprofit organizational ventures. Somers and Somers identified the trends toward more comprehensive medical institutions and systems of care.[48] The advent of Medicare and Medicaid have led public hospitals, such as those administered by New York City's Health and Hospitals Corporation to contract and local voluntary (nonprofit) hospitals to absorb the case loads and in some cases the administration of formerly public facilities.

More commonly, successful nonprofit hospitals, such as Long Island Jewish—Hillside Medical Center in New York, have expanded through merger, that is, by acquiring nearby proprietary facilities or other nonprofits with administrative problems.[49,50] One motivation for such merger activity is the fact that expansion-minded hospitals have faced resistance to new building programs from cost-conscious government officials who believe that there are already too many beds available.[51] Buying up existing capacities circumvents this resistance.

Cost considerations are also a prime factor in the development of prepaid medical care provided by health-maintenance organizations (HMOs). Pioneered by the Kaiser Hospitals in California (see Lehman)[52], HMOs have begun to develop more rapidly with the advent of federal-assistance grants. The new Community Health Plan of Suffolk, the expansion into hospital care by the Health Insurance Plan of Greater New York (HIP), and the Blue Cross HMO in New Hyde Park are recent examples of HMO activity.[53]

The area of law services and legal advocacy provides additional examples of recent nonprofit entrepreneurship, for example, by Ralph Nader in the public-interest law movement. This includes the formation of research institutes, such as the Center for the Study of Responsive Law, and the founding of public interest law firms, gathering momentum around 1970 with support of the Ford Foundation.[54]

The performing arts constitute another broad area of activity where nonprofit entrepreneurship has lately been much in evidence. As reviewed by Nielsen, the number of major opera companies, symphony orchestras, dance companies, and legitimate theaters more than doubled in the 1968–1978 period.[55] Netzer cites the establishment of regional and touring companies, such as the Baltimore Opera Company and Trinity Square Repertory in Providence as significant developments.[56]

Many other examples are cited in the press. The Performing Arts Foundation (PAF) Playhouse in Huntington, New York is one illustration in the field of dramatic performance.[57,58,59] Founded in 1966 by a high-school teacher with a large grant from the U.S. Office of Education, the theater was intended as a medium for arts education and as a community theater for presentation of revivals. By 1974, however, the theater was seriously in debt and threatened with closing. Under the leadership of its board president—folksinger Harry Chapin—and newly appointed director Jay Broad and with substantial help from private foundations, government, and major corporations, PAF was transformed from a local repertory theater into a regional, professional theater which presents primarily original works. Over the period 1975–1978, the budget tripled, subscriptions rose from 2,000 to 14,000, and a new half-million-dollar theater was constructed. Unfortunately, the theater experienced renewed difficulties and folded a few years later, following Mr. Chapin's untimely death.

Other recent examples of nonprofit enterprise in drama include the Arena Stage in Washington, D.C. and the New York Shakespeare Festival in Manhattan. The Oregon Shakespeare Festival reflects nonprofit entrepreneurship on a smaller but no-less-interesting scale.[60] Founded by Angus Bowmer in 1935, it began as a community celebration of the Fourth of July, in Ashland, Oregon, with performances by students and faculty of Southern Oregon State College. The festival now runs a dozen plays per season in three theaters and draws a quarter of a million people.

On Long Island, orchestral music provided an active entrepreneurial context in the late 1970s. Originally two orchestras consisting largely of part-time musicians—The Suffolk Symphony and the Long Island Symphony—served the two counties of Nassau and Suffolk. With impetus from Harry Chapin, a full-time professional orchestra—the Long Island Philharmonic—was formed to replace these two orchestras. The Long Island Symphony, composed of resident musicians, refused to go out of business, however. Disbanded by its board of directors, this orchestra has reorganized as a musicians' cooperative.[61]

Ventures like The Kennedy Center in Washington or the Lincoln Center in New York represent major milestones of interdisciplinary performing-arts enterprise. The Lincoln Center, begun in 1959 under the leadership of John D. Rockefeller, was conceived as an urban redevelopment project that would bring under one roof a "community of the arts."[62] The center has indeed been an ambitious undertaking, now housing The New York Philharmonic Orchestra, the Metropolitan Opera, The New York City Ballet, the Juilliard School of Music, a repertory company, a chamber-music hall, and a library-museum. The Kennedy Center in Washington was envisioned as a national center for the performing arts during the Eisenhower years, but was reconceived as a memorial to John F. Kennedy after 1963. It opened in 1971 and has been developed under the dynamic joint leadership of Roger L. Stevens, board president, and Martin Feinstein, its first executive director.[63,64] Stevens, a lifelong theater entrepreneur, and Feinstein, a trained musician and impresario, are generally recognized to have helped put Washington on the cultural map with top-flight dramatic theater, ballet, music extravaganzas, summer opera, and visiting world-renown opera companies.

Art museums have been one of the most dynamic areas of nonprofit activity in recent years. As Meyer notes:

> Since 1950 the United States has committed at least a half billion dollars to the construction of 10.2 million square feet of art museums and visual art centers, the equivalent footage of 13.6 Louvres.[65]

New museums continued to be founded, often to display art forms not previously provided special recognition. The International Center of Photography in New York City is a recent example, as was the Museum of Modern Art (MOMA) in an earlier era (1929).[66] The recent activity of a group in Los Angeles to found a modern-art facility is an additional illustration.[67]

New museums are often set up to display the private collections of rich men who donate their treasure to the public. The Hirschhorn Museum in Washington, D.C. and the Kimbell Art Museum in Fort Worth (under the leadership of Richard Brown) are important recent examples.[68] Meyer describes additional examples, including the Norton Simon Museum in Pasadena and the Brundage wing of the De Young Museum in San Francisco.[69] The Parrish Museum in Southampton, New York is an older and smaller illustration of the same phenomenon.[70]

Other museums are founded by historically minded entrepreneurs to preserve local treasure. The new art museum (1978) of the Museums at Stony Brook (New York) is devoted to works of the local, renowned nineteenth-century artist William S. Mount. Other museums, like Gallery North in Setauket, New York, which recently converted from proprietary to nonprofit status, are established to display the works of local, living artists.

Within the realm of long-established museums, entrepreneurial activity seems to have taken at least three different directions—the development of new functional subdivisions, the undertaking of commercial ventures to generate financial support, and the creation of popular new exhibitions. An example in the first category is the plan of the Los Angeles County Museum to construct a modern-art wing.[71]

The engagement in commercial sales in support of organizational purposes is a relatively common phenomenon among nonprofits, but some recent initiatives by museums have drawn particular notoriety. In real estate, for example, the Museum of Modern Art in New York has undertaken construction of a forty-four story condominium over a six-story museum building in an effort to generate revenues to offset its increasing operational expenses.[72,73]

The project caused substantial protest, with critics charging that a profit and loss orientation would force the museum to alter its artistic priorities. Other objections included loss of tax revenues to the city and architectural considerations. In a similar vein, museums have enormously increased their activity in the domain of retail sales—for example, memberships that include magazine subscriptions, gift shops, and sale of art reproductions. The larger museums, at least, appear to have learned the lesson taught by Olson, that public goods can be better provided if they are tied in with selective private goods.[74] Hence the receipt of fine magazines (unavailable on newsstands) like The Smithsonian or Natural History or discounts on reproductions of museum pieces increases general-membership support. The Metropolitan Museum of Art reportedly grossed over $16 million in 1978 in commercial revenues (not including memberships and admissions). Smithsonian gift shops drew $7 million, and many other examples can be cited.[75]

The growth in commercial-sales revenue is closely tied to the most spectacular recent museum innovation—the grand exhibition, or supershow, best exemplified by the Metropolitan Museum of Art during the dynamic tenure of Thomas Hoving, with its King Tut (Tutankhamen) tour of 1978.[76] This exhibit was followed at the Metropolitan by other blockbusters, including Pompeii 79, Alexander the Great, and Treasures of the

Kremlin, and by such grand exhibitions as the Cezanne and Picasso shows at the Museum of Modern Art.[77] These large and spectacular shows, often based on foreign-loan collections, have generated considerable revenues for the museums, largely through sales of reproductions and boosted interest in memberships, but they have also generated considerable tension and controversy in the museum world. Seen as a lifeline to rescue museums from the ravages of inflation, the shows are also said to threaten some of the nonprofit museum's basic purposes, such as the discernment of new directions in the art world, art education and research, and other artistic concerns not subject to popular appeal.

As for entrepreneurs in the world of nonprofit museums, the recently deceased Richard Brown and the dynamic Thomas Hoving provide captivating, if very different, examples. Brown was a scholar, teacher, and connoisseur whose desire, according to a colleague, was to "realize an institution that was concerned with excellence, that would provide the finest of visual experiences for the viewer."[78] Hoving, on the other hand, is generally acknowledged to be the most dynamic executive to enter the museum world in many years. A flamboyant entrepreneur, Hoving was characterized by one observer as "A P.T. Barnum."[79] At the Metropolitan Museum of Art, Hoving is credited with securing large, expensive, new collections and controversial art objects, with initiating a major building program that cost more than $70 million and with planning spectacular exhibits like Tutankhamen. Meyer cites several other fascinating entrepreneurial characters in the museum world, including S. Dillon Ripley of the Smithsonian, Francis Henry Taylor of the Metropolitan Museum of Art in the 1940s and 1950s, and Sarah Newmeyer of the Museum of Modern Art, each of whom was responsible for major innovations in museum operations.[80]

In most of the fields reviewed, parallel instances of entrepreneurship can be cited for the profit-making and governmental sectors as well. Proprietary hospitals and nursing homes, government social-service programs, public-education and research initiatives, public museums, and proprietary theater are all rich with contemporary examples. Thus, precisely what factors influence the selection of sector for entrepreneurial activity is not simply a superficial matter of associating a given service with a given economic sector. This question will be explored later in much greater depth.

Nonprofit entrepreneurship is not restricted to the several areas discussed above. Other fields, such as publishing or recreation, provide further illustrations. Some of the most often-cited recent examples of nonprofit entrepreneurship are not easily distinguished from market-oriented commercial ventures. For instance, the new YMCA facility in Washington, D.C. has a sauna, whirlpool, steam room, large pool, and so on and caters to the upper-middle class, with membership fees to match.[81] The Educational Testing Service (ETS) is another nonprofit enmeshed in controversy for its recent market-making behavior.[82] Having grown into an $80 million business, ETS is offering a more diversified set of aptitude and job-placement services, some say at the expense of profit-oriented business competitors. Finally, a venture like Erhard Seminars Training (EST), founded in 1971 by Werner Erhard and boasting a $15 million operation by 1978, has grown on the unique chemistry of evangelism, salesmanship, and a keen eye on what the market will bear for people who can pay to improve themselves.[83]

Nonprofit entrepreneurship is thus a diverse and widespread phenomenon. Yet it has been argued that the nonprofit sector suffers from a lack of entrepreneurship and entrepreneurial talent.[84] In relative terms, this may be true, but there are no adequate measures. What is clear, however, is that entrepreneurship in the nonprofit sector, as elsewhere, represents the cutting edge of the sector's activity, and, as such, its study helps to reveal the driving forces and underlying character of its member organizations.

Of course, entrepreneurship is just one important phase of activity that takes place in an economic sector, and entrepreneurs are just one set of actors who help determine the general patterns of behavior. Certainly, as observed in chapter 9, the motivations, intentions, and circumstances that characterize entrepreneurship may be dissipated over time, as entrepreneurs leave their ventures to successors or as they themselves change or face new exigencies. Furthermore, as discussed in chapter 4, organizations are not only established or grow or change for the better, as normally reflected in entrepreneurship, but they also pass through stages of relative equilibrium and sometimes stagnate or die. These latter aspects of organizational life are also important in establishing overall sector patterns and trends, although it seems plausible that the incidence of entrepreneurship, or lack of it, during periods of organizational uncertainty or stagnation may help account for ultimate survival or demise. Entrepreneurial leadership, or lack of it, can never fully explain why organizations prosper or decline or behave in particular ways. Labor-market trends that affect the cost and availability of particular types of personnel, such as volunteers and paraprofessionals, the cost of other inputs, the nature of societal demands for particular types of goods and services, the alteration of public policies, the demands of labor unions, and the availability of capital may all be beyond entrepreneurial control yet may largely account for global shifts among fields of activity and sectoral shifts within a given field. Still, it may be argued that the manner in which entrepreneurial talent responds or fails to respond to such general changes in context will be highly informative of the vitality and behavior peculiar to particular sectors.

Entrepreneurship is viewed here as an especially useful focal point for attempting to characterize a number of crucial aspects of organizational and sectoral behavior—for example, the extent to which growth, innovation, self-aggrandizing, quality-emphasizing, cost-inflating, socially responsive, market-dominating, or zealously missionary activity are exhibited, or not exhibited, by nonprofit organizations. The reasons for this view are twofold.

First, entrepreneurs are often founding fathers of their organizations, and leaders in their industries. As such, their values and personal motivations for venture will tend to shape in a significant way the organizations that they are establishing or changing. Second, enterprise is the means through which many forms of organizational behavior are exhibited. If an organization is growth oriented, it will grow through enterprising. If it is innovative, it will innovate through new ventures. If it is self-aggrandizing or aspires to market dominance, these goals will be sought largely through the implementation of new enterprise. If such characteristics are lacking, there will be a dearth of entrepreneurial activity.

Still, as noted previously, describing entrepreneurial motives or the nature of enterprising projects alone is insufficient for generalizing to overall patterns of organization behavior. The role of entrepreneurs and the incidence of venture must be placed into a wider perspective in order to discern where entrepreneurship is likely to take place, how it will vary from one context to another, and how it will be shaped and modified by environmental circumstances.

The next chapter begins to address these questions by considering various scenarios by which entrepreneurial activity typically takes place.

Notes

1. The so-called Austrian school of economics is an exception. See Israel M. Kirzner, *Perception, Opportunity and Profit* (Chicago: University of Chicago Press, 1979). See also Israel M. Kirzner, *Competition and Entrepreneurship* (Chicago: University of Chicago Press, 1973).

2. See *Webster's New World Dictionary of the American Language,* College Edition (World Publishing Company, 1968).

3. B.F. Hoselitz, "Entrepreneurship and Economic Growth," *American Journal of Economic Sociology* 12 (1952).

4. Joseph A. Schumpeter, *The Theory of Economic Development* (Cambridge: Harvard University Press, 1949).

5. William D. Angel, "To Make a City: Entrepreneurship on the Sunbelt Frontier," in *The Rise of the Sunbelt Cities*, eds. David C. Perry and Alfred J. Watkins, Urban Affairs Annual Reviews, vol. 14 (Beverly Hills: Sage Publications, 1977).

6. Matthew Josephson, *The Robber Barons* (New York: Harcourt, Brace and World, Inc., 1962).

7. Orvis Collins and David G. Moore, *The Organization Makers*, (New York: Appleton-Century-Crofts, 1970).

8. Alfred Marshall, *Economics of Industry (London: Macmillan and Company, 1964)*.

9. Angel, "Entrepreneurship."

10. Collins and Moore, *Organization Makers*.

11. Schumpeter, *Economic Development*.

12. Authur H. Cole, *Business Enterprise in a Social Setting* (Cambridge: Harvard University Press, 1959).

13. Collins and Moore, *Organization Makers*.

14. Albert O. Hirschman, *Exit, Voice, and Loyalty* (Cambridge: Harvard University Press, 1970).

15. Washington Consulting Group Inc. for the U.S. Jaycees Foundation, *Uplift: What People Themselves Can Do* (Salt Lake City: Olympus Publishing Co., 1974).

16. Dennis R. Young and Stephen J. Finch, *Foster Care and Nonprofit Agencies* (Lexington, Mass.: Lexington Books, D.C. Heath and Company, 1977).

17. Cheryl McCall, "Father Ritter's Mission in Rescuing Runaway Youths from Times Square Sex Peddlers," *People*, November 13, 1978.

18. Aileen Jacobson, "Where Unwanted Boys Find a Family," *Newsday*, August 4, 1979.

19. Maureen Early, "Walking Tall," *Newsday*, November 16, 1978. Also, Henry Viscardi, *A Laughter in the Lonely Night* (New York: Paul S. Eriksson Inc. 1961).

20. Leonard Levitt, "Uncle John," *Newsday*, April 15, 1979.

21. I. Ira Goldenberg, *Build Me a Mountain* (Cambridge: MIT Press, 1971).

22. Mark Moore and Mark Ziering "Methadone Maintenance" (Case study, Kennedy School of Government, Harvard University, 1976).

23. Bruce C. Vladeck, *Unloving Care* (New York: Basic Books, 1980). Burton Dunlop, *The Growth of Nursing Home Care* (Lexington Mass.: Lexington Books, D.C. Heath and Company, 1979).

24. Jacqueline Grennon and Robert Barsky, "Case Studies in Nursing Home Entrepreneurship," (PONPO working paper, Institution for Social and Policy Studies, Yale University, 1980).

25. Vladeck, *Unloving Care*.

26. U.S. Congress, House Select Committee on Aging, Subcommittee on Health and Long-Term Care, *Innovative Alternatives to Institutionalization*, July 8, 1965.

27. William Borders, "Oxfam Takes Only One Side-The Side of the Hungry," *New York Times*, November 4, 1979.

28. Michael T. Kaufman, "The World of Mother Theresa," *New York Times Magazine*, December 9, 1979.

29. Susan Rose-Ackerman, "United Charities: An Economic Analysis" Working paper 822. (Institution for Social and Policy Studies, Yale University, August 1979).

30. Timothy Saasta, "Accusing the Biggest Charity of Greed," *Newsday*, November 26, 1979.

31. Colman McCarthy, "Singing Out for Woody Guthrie," *Newsday*, November 14, 1978.

32. James Barron, "When Churches Get Into the Business of Housing," *New York Times*, May 13, 1979.

33. Waldemar A. Nielsen, *The Big Foundations*, (Twentieth Century Fund, New York: Columbia University Press, 1972).

34. Waldemar A. Nielsen, *The Endangered Sector* (New York: Columbia University Press, 1979).

35. David Riesman and Verne A. Stadtman, eds., *Academic Transformation*, Carnegie Commission on Higher Education (New York: McGraw-Hill, 1973).

36. Donald Stokes, "The Sterling Touch: How Stanford Became a World Class University," *The Stanford Observer*, October 1979.

37. Edward B. Fiske, "N.Y.U., Bucking National Trend, Expands Its Classes and Faculty," *New York Times*, November 26, 1979.

38. Gene I. Maeroff, "Emory U. Seeks New Stature on a Gift and a Dream," *New York Times*, November 18, 1979.

39. Gene I. Maeroff, "Suits Draw Attention to Unorthodox Education Combine," *New York Times*, May 14, 1976.

40. Edward B. Fiske, "Peabody College Approves Merger with Vanderbilt, Ending a Debate," *New York Times*, March 20, 1979.

41. Gene I. Maeroff, "Bard College Taking Over Early-Entrance School," *New York Times*, February 4, 1979.

42. "Some Colleges are Bobbing Up Everywhere," *New York Times*, January 7, 1979.

43. Michael Knight, "Tufts Plans Major New Veterinary School," *New York Times*, April 17, 1979.

44. Edward W. Lehman and Anita M. Waters, "Control in Policy Research Institutes: Some Correlates," *Policy Analysis* (Spring 1979).

45. Paul Dickson, *Think Tanks* (New York: Atheneum, 1971). Also, Bruce L.R. Smith, *The Rand Corporation* (Cambridge: Harvard University Press, 1966).

46. Nielsen, *Endangered Sector*.

47. Linda Field, "Suffolk Hospital Plans Hospice Program," *Newsday*, November 16, 1978.

48. Herman M. Somers and Anne R. Somers, *Medicare and the Hospitals* (Washington, D.C.: Brookings Institution, 1967).

49. Lawrence C. Levy, "Purchase of Hospital Seen Close," *Newsday*, May 27, 1979.

50. Ronald Sullivan, "Roosevelt and St. Lukes Merge Into One Hospital," *New York Times*, October 10, 1979.

51. Lawrence C. Levy, "Glen Cove Hospital Seeks Takeover," *Newsday*, December 26, 1978.

52. Edward W. Lehman, *Coordinating Health Care* (Beverly Hills: Sage Publications, 1975).

53. Neill S. Rosenfeld, "Prepaid Health Plans Flourish on L.I.," *Newsday*, November 25, 1978.

54. Joel F. Handler, Betsy Ginsberg, and Authur Snow, "The Public Interest Law Industry," chapter 4 in *Public Interest Law*, eds. Burton Weisbrod, Joel F. Handler, and Neil Komesar (Berkeley: University of California Press, 1978).

55. Nielsen, *Endangered Sector*.

56. Dick Netzer, *The Subsidized Muse* (New York: Cambridge University Press, 1978).

57. C. Gerald Fraser, "PAF Playhouse 'Grows'," *New York Times*, December 27, 1978.

58. Alvin Klein, "For PAF, Troubles Follow Success," *Newsday*, October 29, 1979.

59. Barbara Delatiner, "A New Theatre Opens and PAF is the Star," *New York Times*, January 7, 1979.

60. Edith Evans Asbury, "Angus L. Bowmer, 74, Founder of Oregon Shakespeare Festival," *New York Times*, May 29, 1979.

61. Barbara Delatiner, "Regrouped L.I. Symphony to Settle in Long Beach," *New York Times*, August 19, 1979.

62. Irving Kolodin, "Lincoln Center at 20: Old Problems, New Initiatives," *Newsday*, May 13, 1979.

63. Tom Prideaux, "The Man Behind Kennedy Center," *Review*, April 1979.

64. Harold C. Schonberg, "A Shock from Kennedy Center," *New York Times*, September 30, 1979.

65. Karl E. Meyer, *The Art Museum* (New York: William Morrow and Co., 1979), p. 13.

66. Hilton Kramer, article on the Museum of Modern Art, *New York Times Magazine*, November 4, 1979.

67. Grace Glueck, "2 New Contemporary Art Museums Are Being Planned for Los Angeles," *New York Times*, October 25, 1979.

68. Grace Glueck, "Richard Fargo Brown Dead at 63: Led Ft. Worth's Kimbell Museum," *New York Times*, November 7, 1979.

69. Karl E. Meyer, *Art Museum*.

70. Amei Wallach, "A Museum Looking to Get Engaged," *Newsday*, July 1, 1979.

71. Glueck, "Contemporary Art Museums."

72. Paul Goldberger, "The New MOMA: Mixing Art with Real Estate," *New York Times Magazine*, November 4, 1979.

73. Grace Glueck, "Modern Museum Head Hopeful Despite Setback from Court," *New York Times*, August 1978.

74. Mancur Olson, *The Logic of Collective Action* (Cambridge: Harvard University Press, 1965).

75. Olivia Buehl, "Museums and the Art of Retail," *Flightime* (Allegheny Airlines, April 1979).

76. Grace Glueck, "The Tut Show Gives a Midas Touch to Almost Everyone but the Viewer," *New York Times*, December 24, 1978.

77. Hilton Kramer, "Has Success Spoiled American Museums?" *New York Times*, January 14, 1979.

78. Glueck, "Richard Fargo Brown."

79. Grace Glueck, "How Fares the Met Museum in the Post-Hoving Era?" *New York Times*, April 8, 1979.

80. Karl E. Meyer, *Art Museum*.

81. Karen De Witt, "Plush New 'Y' Built on Controversy," *New York Times*, April 21, 1979.

82. Edward B. Fiske, "Student Testing Unit's Expansion Leads to Debate," *New York Times*, November 14, 1979.

83. Dave G. Houser, "Is est It?," *Sky* (Delta Airlines, March 1979).

84. Harold S. Williams, "Entreprencurs in the Non-Profit World," *In Business*, July–August, 1980.

4 Circumstances for Venture

Entrepreneurship is a universal process, pervading all sectors and industries of the economy. Despite the variety of contexts in which entrepreneurship occurs, the nature of this process is remarkably similar from one area of experience to another. This chapter describes the generic tasks that entrepreneurial activity entails, the few basic scenarios that ventures tend to follow, and the general conditions of sector development that these scenarios appear to reflect. To use an analogy from chemistry, these latter conditions represent the ambience—the temperature, pressure, and so on—in which entrepreneurial catalysts can be expected to create enterprise from the resources available to them in a given industry and sector.

The Entrepreneurship Process

The similar experiences with organizational and program initiatives and innovation across sectors of the economy reflect a generic process of entrepreneurship. In this process there is generally at least one central figure (the entrepreneur) who catalyzes the venture and ensures its implementation. In Frank Knight's view, the entrepreneur is one who acts on a clear vision in murky circumstances. According to Marris and Mueller, Knight's concept of the entrepreneurial role "is to make decisions under uncertainty and assume responsibility for the consequences of these decisions. To make good decisions in the face of uncertainty requires good information, and so the entrepreneurial role becomes one of gathering, evaluating, and utilizing information."[1] Moreover, the process involves a number of crucial stages or tasks that must be accomplished for venture implementation.

A perusal of the author's case studies reveals these tasks to be quite general, if not uniform in sequence or emphasis from case to case.

Idea Generation. The concept of a particular change or innovation must be articulated. An entrepreneur need not be the originator of the idea—it may even come in the form of a solicitation from an outside agency, for example, a charity or foundation wishing to stimulate a certain type of program—but the entrepreneur must see its relevance to his own situation and he must see to it that the idea is translated from abstraction to application.

Proposal Development. An idea must be clarified and elaborated, a design for implementation must be developed, and resource needs and other implications for the host organization and other participants must be spelled out. A need, or market, for the proposed activity must also be demonstrated. The proposal may be formally written for presentation to outside sources of funds or it may consist of internal communications if the venture is to be supported wholly from within. The entrepreneur may not necessarily be the author of the proposal, for example, he may commission it to be written by a staff member or a consultant, but he will usually initiate this exercise and control its content.

Resource Development. Once a proposal is in circulation it must be sold to those whose resources are needed to support the venture. In the case of a profit-making business, investors or lenders must be found. For nonprofit agencies applications may be made to foundations or to grant-giving government agencies. In government, efforts must be made to secure budget lines or to pass relevant legislation. Some ventures may not require extra resources, or such resources may be available from a budget directly accessible to the entrepreneur. In most cases, however, others have to be convinced of the sensibility of using existing or additional resources to support the venture. Resource development is a key function of the entrepreneur. In some cases, the entrepreneur will rely on influential colleagues to develop resources (for example, an agency director may depend on members of his board of directors for fund raising), but he must always remain abreast of resource possibilities.

Path Clearing. In addition to garnering resources, other institutional barriers often must be overcome to implement a venture. For example, corporate charters, licenses, or other official approvals may have to be secured to operate a particular type of service, manufacture a certain good, or become eligible for a particular source of government funds. Again, much of this work can be delegated, but the overall orchestration, worrying, and crisis handling must be done by the entrepreneur.

Organizing Venture Leadership. Once economic and institutional impediments have been overcome, it is necessary to ensure that the venture be self-sustaining. It must have adequate leadership or management, especially in its early life. Often the entrepreneur will assume this management role for some period of time. Sometimes the entrepreneur will explicity shun the management role. Nonetheless, he must ensure that capable leadership is put in place in order to successfully carry out operations.

Program Development. Even with plans laid, leadership in place, resources available, and necessary permissions obtained, ventures must be organized from within. Staff must be hired, facilities secured and occupied, and equipment purchased. There may be some period of time during which the venture officially exists but is not yet open for business. During this period, which may overlap with the path-clearing and resource-development stages, venture leadership often operates as a small, core staff attempting to put the final pieces in place. In doing so, this group may find that the initial plans (proposal) are vague or require modifications. This is a crucial phase for the venture and requires the entrepreneur's nursing, even if that entrepreneur does not assume management responsibilities.

Overall, there are a number of salient points to be noted about the entrepreneurial process and the specific role of the entrepreneur.

1. The work of implementing a new venture will entail some division of labor among collaborators, staff, consultants, and other colleagues of the entrepreneur. The exact division of labor will vary from case to case, with the entrepreneur assuming direct responsibility for some tasks and sharing or delegating other tasks.

2. Certain core groups may be involved in the process. At the initial stages of proposal and resource development there may be a committee of colleagues or a coalition of interested parties who share in the work. In the later stages, a formal core staff may carry the ball.

3. The entrepreneur may work in a number of different ways—in some cases taking on most of the direct work, in other cases operating behind the scenes to ensure that the work gets done. What distinguishes the entrepreneur from others involved in an entrepreneurial venture is his assumption of the responsibility to make things happen. As Schumpeter indicates, the entrepreneur behaves as a "driving power" and "promoter," doing what is necessary to move a venture from idea to operation.[2]

It would be improper to conclude that the simple presence of an entrepreneur is sufficient to precipitate an entrepreneurial venture. As Shapero states "The (entrepreneurial) event becomes the dependent variable while the individual or group that generates the event become the independent variables, as do the social, economic, political, cultural, and other situational variables."[3] One way to begin to understand this equation is to consider the kinds of events and circumstances that appear to precipitate venture activity.

Stylized Scenarios

Ventures tend to follow a few fairly universal patterns, regardless of the contexts in which they occur. In particular, almost any venture can be described by one of a small set of generic scenarios. These scenarios are shaped by both the personal circumstances of the entrepreneur and the particular social, professional, and organizational context in which he is imbedded. These scenarios also tend to mirror the general economic and social conditions of the sectors and industries in which they take place.

The three basic categories of entrepreneurship scenarios are the initiative, evolutionary, and problem-response modes. The initiative venture mode is the closest in character to the conventional (folklore) image of how entrepreneurs work and follows in linear fashion the steps outlined above for venture implementation. In this mode, an entrepreneur who can bring his own ideas to bear or an entrepreneur who can opportunistically discern and develop a concept that has emerged at the forefront of technology or current professional or political debate may shape and develop that idea into an operating project or program or organizational unit. In cases observed by the author, for example, such ideas include the application of computers to the management of social agencies, the comprehensive diagnosis of children prior to foster-care placement, the control of social agencies by their constituent communities, and the caring for unwed mothers and their babies in a common shelter. In these cases, the entrepreneurs became convinced of the value and feasibility of the new concepts, carefully worked out operational plans, proceeded systematically to convince the relevant authorities, and eventually developed the required resources for implementation.

In a second variation of the initiative mode, the entrepreneur may exploit a unique opportunity to implement an idea that may have been gestating in the back of his mind for some time. When the proper circumstances fall into place, he is thus ready to spring into action. In one observed case, for example, the proposal to merge and integrate two agencies, long talked about and considered, was implemented by seizing on the opportunity created by the retirement of one of the chief executives. More generally, unique grant opportunities often serve as special chances to pursue pending ideas.

The evolutionary mode is an entrepreneurial scenario in which the venture represents more culmination, continuation, or incremental extension of ongoing developments than striking out in a new direction. This mode requires an entrepreneur who operates over the long term by creating a receptive environment and nurturing developments within his purview. Such an entrepreneur may develop his agency like a workshop, greenhouse, or laboratory for ongoing projects. In one variation of the evolutionary mode, the venture arises as the formalization of ongoing internal program developments. In one observed case, for example, the venture consisted of the formal organizing of an already operating volunteer effort to house runaway youths. In another case, it was the structuring and solidifying of existing efforts to provide consultation to a set of child-care agencies by a university group.

In a second type of evolutionary scenario, the venture represents a more discontinuous, yet still incremental, extension of current programmatic developments in response to some unusual opportunity. An illustrative case is that of a children's hospital that took a quantum jump toward emphasis on outpatient care—a direction in which it was already developing—in response to a special grant opportunity. This type of evolutionary scenario bears a strong resemblance to the second initiative mode variation, except that the latter builds on a new idea rather than on a program already in place.

The problem response mode of entrepreneurship is perhaps the most common type of entrepreneurial scenario, although it probably fits the popular conception of entrepreneurship least well. There are two distinct problem-response mode variations—the personal type and the organizational type.

The personal type of problem-response venture is built on an individual's crisis or frustration and represents striking out in a new direction. In this mode the entrepreneur may find his present situation (for example, employment) intolerable, although he may be unsure of what action to take, or he may feel thwarted and frustrated by his superiors and resolve to set out on his own, free from the direct authority of others. In these cases, the personal problem-response mode of venture is inspired by a long-simmering uneasiness that can be triggered by a single event or incident. The individual may be laid off or fired, thereby moving latent entrepreneurial energies to a state of conscious resolve. In other cases, the transition is more gradual, but at some point it gathers a momentum that precludes turning back. Shapero provides a number of private-sector and international examples of the personal problem-response scenario, which he refers to as negative displacement.[4]

The second variation of problem-response mode, the organizational type, involves a venture designed to resolve an organizational crisis. As described in the last chapter, this is the classic turnaround situation. Most commonly, the crisis is financial in nature but is likely to encompass managerial problems, program uncertainties, social pressures, and personnel difficulties as well.

The organizational crisis spells opportunity for entrepreneurs both within the failing agency and outside. From the inside, the crisis may attract those who fear for their organization and are prompted to take action that will save it. The organizational crisis may also be a hunting ground for those internal members who view it as a chance to move up, gain control, seek promotion, or increase their incomes.

Organizational crises are also likely to attract entrepreneurial interest from the outside, especially if the crisis has reached major proportions unresolvable by internal talent. Again, outsiders may view these circumstances as opportunities for gain. One variant here is the merger, whereby a failing organization is absorbed by another agency headed by an entrepreneuring executive. In such cases, the crisis of the failing agency may be resolved, while the resultant expansion of the entrepreneuring agency provides its executive with rewards concomitant with his enlarged responsibilities.

Another possibility is the recruitment of fresh talent to the suffering organization. This situation is most likely to occur when the organization has good prospects for recovery. For example, the agency may have a large but eroding endowment, substantial latent capital resources, or other hidden potential, which, if properly used or converted, might turn the agency around. In such circumstances, an entrepreneur from outside might agree to join the failing agency if provided with assurances that he will be able to make the changes he thinks are required, will be adequately rewarded for succeeding, and will have a free hand in reshaping the agency and running it thereafter.

Sector Conditions

The three modes of venture scenario reflect, in an approximate way, different underlying conditions in the industrial environment as a whole. The initiative mode, for example, presupposes a degree of ferment in the economic, professional, or social context, perhaps stimulated by demographic, technological, and economic shifts and trends, generating ideas and opportunities for change. Thus at any one time some industries are more likely than others to experience the initiative mode of entrepreneurship. Those industries would be characterized by a high level of questioning of conventional methods and practices. For example, treatment methods such as institutional care in the social- and health-service areas may be challenged by research and professional debate that casts doubt on the effectiveness of that care and indicates that preventive or community-based strategies might be more viable, thus creating ideas for entrepreneurs to develop and pursue.

The evolutionary mode of entrepreneurship nominally requires relatively stable and prosperous environmental conditions in which ideas and projects are gradually encouraged and nurtured. These ideas and projects arise from adaptive solutions to long-term problems (such as treatment of diseases) or from the maturing of professional ideas, not from social, economic, or intellectual tumult. Evolutionary ventures grow in a tolerant and protective environment, within relatively mature and stable progressive organizations led by innovative (entrepreneurial) managers or managers who delegate considerable discretion to innovative senior staff. Thus evolutionary ventures will be found most commonly in fields of endeavor that feature a professional ethic of cautious progress and in sectors within those industries populated by mature, professionally oriented organizations with the resources and managerial patience to nurture projects over time.

The problem-response mode of entrepreneurship occurs in sectors and industries that exhibit high levels of obsolescence, perhaps because of their age or because they have been outpaced by external events. For example, ventures based on response to personal problems are often rooted in the failure of some organizations to respond to the yearnings of young, latent entrepreneurs. If such stultifying circumstances are peculiar to a particular organization, the prospective entrepreneur may find satisfaction by moving to another agency in the same sector and industry. If most agencies in that category are similarly problematic, the prospective entrepreneur may try to form a new agency, or he may switch sectors or industries, for example from government to the nonprofit sector or from education to camping for handicapped children. Thus ventures of the personal problem-response variety may begin in sectors and industries that are relatively stagnant and move into sectors with more flexible and forward-looking conditions.

Ventures of the organizational problem-response type are even more germane to industries that have large numbers of troubled agencies. In contrast to the personal problem-response mode, the organizational variety of problem-response venture is inspired and usually resolved within that same sector. (An interesting but relatively small set of exceptions includes organizations that change sectors, such as profit-making firms that become nonprofit in order to resolve their financial difficulties. See Hutchins.)[5] Furthermore, the organizational problems that lead to venture activity are likely to be much more severe and immediate in the organizational problem-response case. Not only may the organizations at issue experience stagnation, but they may be well on their way to bankruptcy and dismemberment. Industries where economic or social events have outstripped organizations' abilities to adapt or keep pace are good places to look for ventures of an organizational problem-response type. Older sectors with stagnant personnel structures or tenure systems within such industries are likely possibilities. Sectors that feature organizations with financial cushions, such as historic endowments in the nonprofit case, access to entrenched tax levies in government, or capital reserves of large corporations, constitute another target area. In the former case, the lack of new blood allows organizations to fall behind and eventually lose vigor and control. In the latter case, the financial cushion allows organizations to postpone facing the facts of changing economic environments (inflation, changes in demand and cost structures) until it is too late. These are classic cases of organizations that have built up inordinate margins of slack, which, in Albert Hirchman's analysis, causes them to become unresponsive to their environments until they are in serious trouble.[6] Many universities, social agencies, and other nonprofits have been caught in this bind. The cases of Lockheed, Chrysler,

New York City, and Cleveland attest to the fact that the condition is not unique to the nonprofit sector, however.

Sector Maturity

In a rough sense, the initiative, evolutionary, and problematic scenarios of venture reflect different states of development or evolution of an economic sector. The initiative mode is easily associated with a vibrant, expanding new industry or with the renewal of an older but still vigorous industry facing new conditions. The evolutionary mode correlates with a more mature and stable, but prosperous, sector in which an equilibrium or steady growth pattern has been achieved. The problematic mode is more easily associated with a troubled, decaying or contracting sector, where the demand for traditional services has declined or cost pressures or quality problems have made services difficult to deliver.

The correlation between enterprise scenarios and sector conditions is highly imperfect. Organizational failures do take place in dynamic and prospering sectors, and organizational successes are maintained in the worst of conditions. Nevertheless, ambient sector conditions may serve as a crude indicator of the relative occurrences of the three types of enterprise scenarios, and the growth and decline of sectors may be signaled by the natural history of its member organizations. As noted by various scholars, including Hirschman,[7] Downs,[8] and Mueller,[9] individual organizations tend to pass through similar sequences of development, albeit with different cyclical periods and different ultimate outcomes. Organizations are born, and they struggle to survive. If they surmount the problems of birth, they often enter a dynamic growth phase, which at some point tends to level off and settle into a relatively stable equilibrium. Ultimately, an internal loss of vigor or a failure to adapt to new environmental circumstances may occur, resulting in deterioration. This process, according to Hirschman, is the result of a natural buildup of entropy, or slack. If circumstances are right, the organization may recover from its decline and enter a new period of stability or growth. If decline is not suitably addressed, the organization will wither and may eventually become defunct.

Nielsen gives an example of such evolution for social-action movements, which sometimes develop into formal corporate entrepreneurial ventures.

> Some [movements] are born out of circumstances of mass excitement or unrest, carry on their efforts for a period, and subsequently disappear, having achieved their mission or having lost their motivation and following. Some begin as ardent reformers, evolve into more formal structures, and eventually become sedate operating entities, fulfilling their cause in the performance of a conventional function.[10]

Given the generic tendencies of organizations to follow such historical patterns of maturation, the age of a given sector, obviously correlated with the age of its member agencies, will be suggestive of the types of opportunities for venture that it contains. (See Mueller.)[11] Newer sectors, featuring organizations struggling to survive and establish themselves on the basis of new concepts or services, will more likely reflect opportunities in the initiative mode. Established sectors, featuring prospering organizations, will feature the evolutionary mode. Aging sectors will more likely reflect the problematic scenarios.

An interesting and important question is why different sectors within the same industry tend to develop at different times and why, at any given point in time, alternate sectors present different opportunities for entrepreneurial ventures. James Douglas reviews this phenomenon in a recent paper.[12] He argues (in contrast to the government and market-failure theories of Weisbrod and Hansmann, respectively) that "Historically, most activities . . . have originally been in what we are calling the Third (nonprofit) Sector, and the activities still remaining there are those in which neither the market sector nor the government sector have enjoyed a sufficient advantage to draw them out of the Third Sector."

In the broad scan of development in certain fields such as charity and social service or education, this account seems accurate. Voluntary nonprofit institutions developed early as self-contained, cooperative efforts of communities to accommodate their own needs. Where profit opportunities arose in that context and were permitted to develop, that sector later grew. Where the larger public viewed private activity (both voluntary and profit) as insufficient, government initiatives were taken. The sequence is not fixed, however. Hospitals have shown a zigzag pattern of public, profit, and nonprofit initiatives; for medical schools, nonprofits have replaced earlier proprietary forms.[13] In nursing homes, a surge of profit making has followed on a mixed proprietary and nonprofit base.[14] Public programs were built after earlier nonprofit efforts in foster care,[15] similar to the pattern for universities.[16] More recently, in fields such as mental health care and criminal corrections, there has been a resurgence of interest in private, nonprofit alternatives, following a long period of governmental dominance.[17] Thus there is no single sequence of sector development across fields, but it does seem apparent that sectors in any industry tend not to develop simultaneously. The result is a differential pattern of venture opportunity across sectors, in any field at any point in time. Furthermore, the zigzag pattern tends to suggest a closure between differential sector development and the natural history of organizations. In particular, in an aging industry dominated by one relatively ossified sector, a new development, such as an innovative technology, change in service demand, or social problem, may stimulate (initiative mode) entrepreneurship outside the dominant sector as much as it may inspire (problem-solving mode) entrepreneurship inside that sector.

Summary

The ambient, historically derived conditions of an economic sector roughly mirror the patterns of enterprise that transpire within it.

New industries, or still-vibrant sectors inspired by fundamental changes in social conditions or technology, will tend to feature initiative-mode scenarios, with entrepreneurs who can quickly capitalize on emergent ideas and convert them into operating ventures.

Established and prospering sectors will tend to feature evolutionary-mode scenarios, with entrepreneurs who can cultivate organizational environments in which programmatic developments may be continually nurtured over time.

Aging, rigidifying sectors that have become seriously out of tune with social and economic conditions may give rise to both problematic and initiative modes of venture scenario. In particular, aging sectors in changing environments may inspire initiative-mode developments in adjacent sectors by failing to internally accommodate entrepreneurial energies and by ultimately encouraging entrepreneurs to exploit opportunities elsewhere. Just as commonly, however, declining sectors will feature struggling organizations that become the focal point both of inside entrepreneurs, who attempt to rescue their agencies, and of outsiders, who see opportunities for resurrection and gain amid the decay.

The discussion in this chapter strongly implies that the various venture scenarios tend to engage entrepreneurs with a number of different reasons and motives for undertaking enterprising activity. The next chapter describes the essential nature of these entrepreneurial drives.

The discussion also suggests that current economic and social conditions in a sector affect the kinds of entrepreneurial motivations attracted to those opportunities as well as the frequency with which venture opportunities manifest themselves. Theory must necessarily deal with these phenomena in simplified and indirect ways. Potential entrepreneurs of different persuasions will be seen to distribute themselves among sectors of the economy at early points in their careers according to what they perceive to be the current and likely future attributes of those sectors. Assessment of some of these attributes will obviously be influenced by ambient sector conditions and states of development. For example, career decisions will be seen to hinge on the public importance attached to alternative industries and to the relative employment opportunities available in particular sectors of an industry, characteristics clearly tied to the current status and history of development of these parts of the economy. Furthermore, the theory will recognize that activation of the energies of entrepreneurs previously channeled into a particular sector will depend on current conditions in that sector. In particular, entrepreneurs will be seen to operate within a set of opportunities and constraints that implicitly depend on the sector's state of development. Beyond these general parameters, the theory must ignore the complexities of chronological development and changes in the ambient conditions of sectors and industries, in the hope that the resulting simplification will pay off in terms of clarity, without sacrificing too much realism.

Notes

1. Robin Marris and Dennis C. Mueller, "The Corporation, Competition, and the Invisible Hand," *Journal of Economic Literature*, March 1980.

2. Joseph A. Schumpeter, *The Theory of Economic Development* (Cambridge: Harvard University Press, 1949).

3. Albert Shapero, "Some Social Dimensions of Entrepreneurship" (Draft, Ohio State University, presented to Conference on Entrepreneurship Research, Baylor University, March 1980).

4. Shapero, "Dimensions of Entrepreneurship."

5. Dexter C. Hutchins, "The Nonprofit Alternative," *Venture Magazine*, June 1980.

6. Albert O. Hirschman, *Exit, Voice and Loyalty* (Cambridge: Harvard University Press, 1970).

7. Hirschman, *Voice and Loyalty*.

8. Anthony Downs, *Inside Bureaucracy* (Boston: Little Brown and Co., 1966).

9. Dennis C. Mueller, "A Life Cycle Theory of Firms," *Journal of Industrial Economics* (July 1972).

10. Waldemar Nielsen, *The Endangered Sector* (New York: Columbia University Press, 1979).

11. Mueller, Life Cycle.

12. James Douglas, "Towards a Rationale for Private Non-Profit Organizations" (PONPO working paper 7, Institution for Social and Policy Studies, Yale University, April 1980).

13. Nielsen, *Endangered Sector*.

14. Bruce C. Vladeck, *Unloving Care* (New York: Basic Books, 1980).

15. David M. Schneider and Albert Deutsch, *The History of Public Welfare in New York State: 1867–1940* (Chicago: University of Chicago Press, 1941).

16. Nielsen, *Endangered Sector*.

17. For example, see Yitzhak Bakal and Howard W. Polsky, *Reforming Corrections for Juvenile Offenders* (Lexington, Mass.: Lexington Books, D.C. Heath and Company, 1979).

5 Models of Entrepreneurs

Whereas the tasks and scenarios around which new ventures develop are quite general, the particular skills, personality traits, styles, and motivations of entrepreneurs can vary substantially. Schumpeter offers one view in his description of the entrepreneur in the profit-making sector:

> the personality of the capitalistic entrepreneur need not, and generally does not, answer to the idea most of us have of what a "leader" looks like, so much so that there is some difficulty in realizing that he comes within the sociological category of leader at all. He "leads" the means of production into new channels. But this he does, not by convincing people of the desirability of carrying out his plan or by creating confidence in his leading in the manner of a political leader—the only man he has to convince or impress is the banker who is to finance him—but by buying them or their services, and then using them as he sees fit.[1]

It is doubtful that this is a wholly adequate description even of the modern profit-making entrepreneur, especially in the context of the large, modern corporation. Nevertheless, the distinction between market-oriented and people-oriented entrepreneuring is useful. The political skills of leadership may be much more important in the public and nonprofit sectors than they are in the profit sector. In the former sectors, it is often not possible and certainly not sufficient to demonstrate to one's banker that a new concept will sell. Furthermore, the trust that the nonprofit or public entrepreneur can engender in his sponsors is often important because the promised results of the new service, methods, and so on will be much harder for sponsors to judge without a market test. Thus sponsors presumably must be confident of the entrepreneur's intentions.

The differences in entrepreneurial skills required in different sectors and industries may correspond to psychological characteristics identified in entrepreneurs by David McClelland.[2] Specifically, McClelland describes achievement-oriented, power-oriented, and affiliation-oriented individuals. Private-sector entrepreneurs are found to be achievement oriented, judging themselves by concrete indicators of accomplishment rather than recognition by, or control of, others:

> the need to achieve . . . was one of the keys to economic growth, because men who are concerned with doing things better have become active entrepreneurs and have created the growing business firms which are the

55

foundation stones of a developing economy. . . . Some of these heroic
entrepreneurs might be regarded as leaders in the restricted sense that their
activities established the economic base for the rise of a new type of
civilization, but they were seldom leaders of men.

Entrepreneurs in the nonprofit and public sectors are also achievers,
but, often not to the exclusion of interests in power and affiliation, because
the latter interests are closely associated with enjoying and working effectively with people. Indeed, McClelland recognizes that "studying the power
motive may help us understand managerial, societal, or even political leadership better," particularly the need for "socialized power," which "is
characterized by a concern for group goals, for finding those goals that will
move men, for helping the group formulate them, for taking some initiative
in providing members of the group with the means of achieving such goals."

It seems clear that entrepreneurs in any context are achievers in some
sense and that they possess certain rare talents of promoting ideas and
organizing people and resources. What is less clear are the underlying
personal objectives of such achievement, energy, and application of skills.
Why do entrepreneurs choose to do what they do? Few scholars have really
probed this question, although it seems relevant to the character that entrepreneurs impart to the organizations and projects that they nurture.
Because the literature on entrepreneurs is thin, this discussion draws on
studies of other classes of organizational participants as well as on some
studies of entrepreneurs.

Chapter 2 noted Weisbrod's study of lawyers of equal credentials who
chose to work for nonprofit rather than profit firms and Hansmann's theory
of entrepreneurial screening between the profit and nonprofit sectors. Weisbrod implies two kinds of motivations—income enhancement and public
spiritedness, as manifested in legal work directed to social causes. Hansmann also implies dual motivations—income and professional pride, as
reflected in the quality of the institution one manages.

Cornuelle cites the desire to serve as helping differentiate the nonprofit
sector:

> In the commercial sector, the motivation is the desire for profit. In the
> government sector, the motivation is the desire for power. . . . But in the
> independent sector, the motivation in its purest form, is the desire to serve
> others. . . .
>
> Whether the desire to serve arises from self-denial or egomania,
> it is a compelling drive.[3]

Vroom, in his study of work and motivation, also notes both the economic and noneconomic motivations of organizational participants, including entrepreneurs:

The evidence concerning noneconomic incentives to work is not restricted to people's reports of their motivations. The existence of "dollar a year men," who work with only token economic rewards and entrepreneurs who continue to work after having amassed tremendous fortunes, is well known.[4]

Vroom also cites Miller and Form, who observe:

The motives for working cannot be assigned only to economic needs—for men may continue to work even though they have no need for material goods. Even when their security and that of their children is assured, they continue to labor. Obviously, this is so because the rewards they get from work are social, such as respect and admiration from their fellow man.

In his study of voluntary organizations in the political area (that is, in Hansmann's terminology, mutual-donative nonprofits such as lobby groups), Wilson also cites a variety of economic and noneconomic incentives for participation by members.[5] These encompass material compensation, including monetary benefits of various kinds, specific intangible rewards such as honors, offices, and personal deference, social satisfactions such as the camaraderie, conviviality and general prestige associated with membership, and purposive satisfaction associated with achievement of the organization's formal social or political goals. Presumably such motives pertain to entrepreneurs as well as to general members of such organizations, although just what distinguishes the entrepreneur is somewhat unclear. Wilson suggests that entrepreneurs may have an exaggerated sense of their likely efficacy, that is, the probability that they can lead the organization to fulfill its formal goals, or they may have an exceptional commitment to such purpose.

The commitment to purpose and to change is what Winter seems to have in mind in describing at least one brand of achievement-oriented innovators:

A careful study of the Puritan impulse towards reform . . . suggests that . . . radical innovators, who are possessed of a transcendental concern for change and excellence (i.e. achievement needs), have always been bitterly attacked by their contemporaries as a small minority of dissident disrupters. . . .

Because of their fundamental needs for achievement, rather than power, these new radicals can be understood as Puritans. They call for a quasi-religious enthusiasm for animation of the individual person, who is then a directed agent of radical social change.[6]

Economic, social, and substantive policy and service motivations (beliefs) all fall within the spectrum of forces that drive entrepreneurial behavior. As Winter notes, however, another consideration is what is commonly referred to as power. McClelland and Watson have studied the power drive, which they distinguish from achievement motivation:

Recent studies . . . support the conclusion that the incentive for a power-oriented person is to "have impact," to "stand out" in some way, or to be considered important. He may pursue this incentive in a variety of ways—by trying to win arguments . . . by collecting prestige possessions . . . by nurturing others, by being aggressive, or even by drinking to increase fantasies of personal power . . . [by] doing well at a task, the achievement incentive, but only in a public situation where others will notice the superior performance and probably only where the person can stand out relative to others—that is, can be judged *superior* to others.[7]

In some contrast to the foregoing highly directed and purposive types of motivations, some scholars have identified other, less delineated or more groping varieties of personal motives for ventures. Shapero, for example, observes the valued autonomy and independence of the street hawker, and the search for these goals by employees frustrated by their organizations.[8] In a related observation Shapero also notes that there are both one-time and chronic entrepreneurs. Having achieved independence or resolved a personal search, a given individual may venture no longer. For others, however, the seeking of power, material reward, or other objectives may be ongoing.

The panoply of motivations that may enter the organization member's (and entrepreneur's) calculus, has been conceptualized by some authors into sets of stereotypical managerial and entrepreneurial actors. A recent effort of this kind is Maccoby's study of corporate leaders in the profit-making sector, *The Gamesman*.[9] In this work, based on several hundred psychological interviews of managers in growth-oriented technology-based corporations, the author identifies four types of managers, two of which normally exhibit entrepreneurial behavior. These are as follows.

The craftsman is motivated by the "pleasure in building something better" and derives his satisfaction directly from the quality of the product that he is responsible for producing. Maccoby includes some corporate scientists in the category of craftsman, but he puts other scientists in a different category, which he discusses only briefly because of their sparcity in the ranks of management. According to Maccoby, "What most distinguishes (these) 'scientists' from the craftsman is their narcissism, their idolatry of their own knowledge . . . and their hunger for admiration: They are the corporate intellectuals."

The jungle fighter lusts for power, derives pleasure from crushing opponents, fears defeat, and wants only to be number one. Maccoby identifies two subtypes of jungle fighter. "The lions are the conquerors who . . . may build an empire; the foxes make their nests in the corporate hierarchy and move ahead by stealth and politicking."

The company man also fears failure, desires approval by authority, and finds his sense of identity by being part of the "powerful, protective company." The company man is thus committed to maintaining the organization's integrity.

The gamesman derives satisfaction from the process of competition. He "responds to work and life as a game . . . enjoys new ideas, new techniques, fresh approaches and short cuts." As with the jungle fighter, but for different psychological reasons, "his main goal in life is to be a winner."

In Maccoby's view, the jungle fighter represents the old-style entrepreneur, the post–Civil War robber barons, such as Andrew Carnegie. The gamesman represents the more civilized, slick, and in many ways more sophisticated modern-day equivalent, the source of dynamism for the large corporation in the complex, governmentally regulated world of the 1960s and 1970s. The craftsman and the company man are more conservative types, lacking the interest or daring for major entrepreneurial ventures. As discussed below, however, some traits of the craftsman and the company man, and even Maccoby's denigrated scientist, are relevant to entrepreneuring in the nonprofit world and in the proprietary and public sectors in industries where nonprofits participate. The craftsman, for example, represents pride and accomplishment in the quality of programs or organizational design. Aspects of the scientist may be seen in some entrepreneuring individuals who seek recognition for their leadership in professional disciplines. Finally, the company man may represent loyalty to cherished traditions that can underlie entrepreneuring behavior designed to rescue failing institutions (in the problem-response mode).

The stereotype approach is also used by Downs to describe styles and motivations of officials who populate the ranks of public bureaucracies.[10] Again, a subset of these seem more inclined toward entrepreneurial behavior, yet each type might be so motivated in the appropriate circumstances. Downs's characters are divided into purely self-interested and mixed motive categories. The self-interested types are climbers, who "consider power, income, and prestige as nearly all-important in their value structures," and conservers, who consider convenience and security as nearly all-important.

The mixed-motive types are zealots, who are "loyal to relatively narrow policies or concepts" and who "seek power both for its own sake and to effect the policies to which they are loyal"; advocates, who are "loyal to a broader set of functions or to a broader organization. . . . They. . . seek power because they want to have a significant influence upon policies and actions concerning those functions or organizations . . . "; and statesmen, who are "loyal to society as a whole and . . . desire to obtain the power necessary to have a significant influence upon national policies and actions. They are altruistic to an important degree because their loyalty is to the 'general welfare' as they see it."

Downs's climbers resemble Maccoby's jungle fighters and gamesmen; his conservers and, perhaps, advocates are breeds of company men. The mixed-motive types are especially interesting. They acknowledge that, although some people may be exclusively self-interested, others are something of a mix. More important, this category provides recognition that beliefs and loyalties to purposes larger than one's self are a genuine source of motivation to participants in organizations. Downs's analysis is directed to the public sector, but such motivations are often strong in the nonprofit sector as well.

To proceed analytically with the present investigation of entrepreneurial behavior, there are essentially three options. One is to recognize that man is a complex, adaptive, and dynamic creature whose motivations are mixed and changing. Thus an entrepreneur may be characterized as having some combination of motives that may vary as he grows older, gains experience, and meets new circumstances. Furthermore, the motivation mix varies from individual to individual. This assumption clearly conforms closely to reality, but is cumbersome for developing analytical models capable of producing incisive and unambiguous hypotheses and insights.

A second approach, popular among economists, is to assume that all men are basically the same and may be characterized by some specific static set of objectives that enter a common utility function. Better yet is to assume that a single motive, such as income maximization, prevails. An intermediate approach is to identify instrumental or proxy variables that capture various entrepreneurial goals in a single index. For example, Niskanen's notion of budget maximizing is intended to represent a package of status, power, and income seeking by bureaucrats.[11] Another example is found in the theory of managerial discretion presented by Williamson and others.[12] According to this theory the corporate manager in the private sector is assumed to maximize his own utility. The arguments of the postulated utility function include a few key variables, such as organizational staff and emoluments, that proxy the status, income, and power objectives.

The single-objective or proxy-utility approach allow analytical (mathematical) elegance and simplicity but are rejected here as strategies for characterizing the behavior of nonprofit entrepreneurial activity. For one thing, these models are exclusively focused on managers, yet entrepreneurs need not always become managers of their enterprises. Indeed, entrepreneurs sometimes develop their ventures with the specific intent of turning them over for others to administer. In addition, empirical observation suggests that entrepreneurial motivations are quite varied and not easily captured by one or two proxy indices such as staff, emoluments, or surplus revenues. The monolithic utility approach puts the entire burden of explaining differences in economic behavior on environmental parameters and incentives structures such as laws and prices by assuming no variations among men. Although this approach may simplify the study of alternative institutional arrangements, it is incapable of recognizing some potentially important implications for social behavior that are based on differential response to environmental factors or policy variables. For example, a model that focuses solely on monetary incentives is valid only if it can be shown that individuals not singularly devoted to profit have been weeded out, (that is, that the relevant world consists only of those actors of a given motive). Otherwise, such a model will fail to account for the behavior of individuals motivated by other factors and relatively indifferent to monetary gain. In the nonprofit and public sectors, it is unreasonable to assume that a single, or even uniform, mix of motives is manifest, hence a monolithic utility model seems inappropriate. Even in the profit sector, as noted in chapter 2, more traditional economic scholars such as Williamson [13] and behaviorists such as Simon [14] and Cyert and March [15] have recognized the significance of the multipart, diverse nature of corporate management.

Many economists do argue that in the competitive, profit-making sector any variety of entrepreneurial or managerial motives is unimportant because those who choose not to emphasize profits will be driven out of business. This argument is hedged in the case of a less than perfectly competitive profit sector by those of the managerial-discretion school, who offer the notion that, whereas profitseeking remains of paramount importance, profit levels above some acceptable minimum may be traded by management for items of personal utility. This idea has even been extended to the public sector by Roger Parks and Elinor Ostrom, who model the public-sector official as exchanging a certain level of net public benefits (called a benefits residuum) for personal utility as proxied by staff levels. [16]

In the nonprofit sector, there is certainly a large margin of entrepreneurial discretion, and nothing closely resembles a profit criterion or a benefits residuum to which entrepreneurs are strongly held by market, political, or other external forces. (See chapter 8.) This is not to say that nonprofit entrepreneurs face no constraints or that they are completely unaccountable for their actions; rather, the sources of accountability and constraint on ventures are so variable, diverse, and diffuse as to allow for a wide spectrum of possible motivations and resulting behaviors.

It may be argued that much of what is called entrepreneurship constitutes attempts to change, rather than play by the existing rules and environmental constraints. For example, in the commercial sector, firms try to take control of, rather than respond to, prevailing price structures, perhaps so that they may comfortably indulge in pursuits other than pure profit making. In the public and nonprofit sectors, the desire for new legislation or new sources of funds also reflects the desires of entrepreneurs to change the environmental parameters that confine their abilities to pursue a variety of motivations. Simply assuming that entrepreneurs with some fixed set of objectives will maximize these objectives subject to accepted constraints often misses the point, that is, it ignores the dynamic element involved in achieving the social or economic change desired by entrepreneurs. Hence, a theory based on entrepreneurship inherently conflicts with the constrained-optimization approach of neoclassical economics and requires more of a behavioral framework in which innovation and rule- and process-changing activity is explicitly recognized.[17]

A third approach to the investigation of entrepreneurial behavior is to recognize the diversity of motivations by postulating alternative stereotypes, in the manner of Maccoby and Downs. This approach is qualitatively different from specifying a single utility function, even one that incorporates a variety of competing objectives, because it recognizes that given motivations and styles may be distributed differently among individuals in the relevant entrepreneurial population and may be pursued in different ways. It thus allows for alternative types of entrepreneurs pursuing different goals and following different organizational paths in their ventures, thereby providing a fuller and more meaningful interpretation of the screening process as well as the behavior that results once different types are sorted into different environments.

The stereotype approach falls short of complete realism also, especially if one tries to associate particular characterizations with actual people. People do change motivations over time, and they do adapt to environmental circumstances in a manner that may even fundamentally alter their values. Sociologists argue that people are malleable and have a tendency to fulfill expectations associated with the (work-related) roles they happen to occupy at any given time. Although this observation clearly contains some truth, it does not answer some questions posed here. For example, why do potential entrepreneurs select particular fields and employment opportunities in the first place, and why do they subsequently act to change the parameters and circumstances of their employment over time? The answers to these questions require explanation based on relatively stable personality traits. Ascribing too much adaptive dynamism to the stereotype models would hopelessly complicate them and make them ineffectual for analytical purposes.

The theory that follows begins with a set of entrepreneurial personality types that are defined independently of environment, although particular manifestations of behavior of these personality types may be strongly environment related. Thus a mission-oriented entrepreneurial type may not find his cause until he has gained the benefit of work experience in a particular field, yet he may still be a generic believer, who is drawn to a given industry or sector because of its ability to accommodate zealous personalities and causes. Alternatively, certain potential entrepreneurs may choose fields of employment for reasons other than personality but may subsequently behave according to the motives inherent in their personal makeup. Although this theory leans to the former process, it also explores the implications of such imperfections in the sorting-by-personality process. I will proceed by postulating stereotype models that seem to capture the alternative driving motivations and styles of entrepreneurs across a wide spectrum of economic activity and that ultimately appear relevant to the association of these entrepreneurs with particular industries, sectors, and venture types. These models derive from observations from the author's field studies and from the literature cited above. Later I will analyze how these entrepreneurial types are screened at the industry and sector levels and derive implications from this process for organization and sector behavior.

It is important to emphasize that the following models are pure types in the sense that each personifies a particular variety of internal motives and drive. Again, actual people are probably more easily thought of in terms of combinations of the postulated models; the models are simply analytical devices to help derive more aggregate behavioral implications for sectors and industries. This approach is possible because the observable aggregate effects of large differentiated populations of pure versus mixed types should be essentially similar, that is, viewed as a whole, it is hard to distinguish populations that contain a wide variety of mixed types from those that contain an equivalent variety of pure types. Thus analysis can proceed as if the world were populated with distributions of pure stereotypical entrepreneurs, although the screening effects considered in chapters 6 and 7 are likely to lead to more homogeneous groupings of entrepreneurial sub-populations for pure types and hence to more exaggerated differences in predicted behavior among sectors and industries. Hence this theory will predict behavior patterns that may actually be harder to detect and isolate empirically than they are to distinguish in the world of conceptual models. The postulated entrepreneurial stereotype models are listed below.

The *artist* is an entrepreneur who derives his satisfaction directly from the creative act and from pride in his own organizational and programmatic constructions. There are basically two types of artists.

The *architect*, a close relation of Maccoby's craftsman, is a builder and tinkerer who likes to play with organizational "blocks." He may view his organization as a workshop for building better structures, both physical and organizational. In one observed case, for example, the entrepreneur took special pride in having reconstructed and nurtured a small, faltering agency into a multicampus, computerized operation with a unique umbrellalike organizational structure.

The *poet* is a less structured and less meticulous, more cerebral and emotional artistic entrepreneur whose creations consist of implemented ideas. Poets may view their agendas as blank canvases or unwritten books to be filled with paintings or stories of their own philosophic conceptions.

Both types of artist like to create, to nurture, and to see things grow. Some, like Angus Bowmer, who founded the Oregon Shakespeare Festival, apparently combine the workmanship concerns of the architect with the emotive feelings of the poet, indulging both a love of acting and a dedication to artistic excellence.[18] Both types seek artistic expression and require the freedom to pursue their work in a relatively unharnessed setting, without restrictive monitoring.

The *professional*, a distant cousin of Maccoby's scientist, is formally trained in a discipline, and is highly attuned to the controversies and debates that characterize his professional domain. He is committed to the standards and methodological approaches of his profession, which may vary in style from the highly scientific character of medicine to the more subjective, theory-oriented, and discursive intellectual modes of social work or education. The professional pursues ventures at the leading edge of current professional thinking in his discipline, and looks to his peers in that discipline as the source of reenforcement, recognition, and acclaim. Elements of this kind of motivation are strongly illustrated in the observed cases where, for example, profession-oriented entrepreneurs have experimented in a careful, calculated manner with such leading-edge concepts as outpatient clinical services for autistic children and common-shelter care for unmarried mothers and babies. Nielsen[19] and Vladeck[20] both cite hospitals and medical care as a domain in which scientifically-oriented manifestations of professional-type motivations are particularly strong.

The *believer*, a relation of Downs's zealot, is an entrepreneur who is unshakably devoted to a cause and consistently formulates his ventures and focuses his energies in pursuit of that cause over a long period of time. He has what Cornuelle calls the service motive, which "is at least as powerful as the desire for profit or power. We see some people in whom it is paramount and overwhelming."[21] The believer's cause may be defined as help for a particular (needy) constituency, it may be a civil-libertarian or social-justice concept, or it may be a particular strategy of social reform, or the believer may simply have a deep, general religious resolve to be of service. Examples abound. Thomas Kielty Scherman founded the Little Orchestra Society and subsidized it from his own personal fortune in order to present what he considered to be important revivals, rare works, new music, and unheralded masterpieces.[22] Ralph Nader is perhaps the quintessential believer, combining a missionary zeal with an ethic of personal sacrifice in his consumer and public-interest law activities.[23]

The *searcher* is restless and frustrated, out to prove himself and to find his niche in the world. He may be a relatively young person, with some job experience, perhaps even moderately successful in what he is doing, but unhappy and critical in his present employment and anxious to resolve the tensions between his aspirations and uncertain self-confidence. Searchers often shun security to find opportunites that will better satisfy their yearnings for career satisfaction. In some cases, however, the searcher may be trying to resolve a mid-life crisis and attach to an institutional structure that provides a new source of identity or security. (See Shapero, for example.)[24] Having found such a solution through some entrepreneurial venture, the searcher may cease to engage in ventures thereafter. A few searchers, however, may be chronic, constantly becoming disillusioned with one venture experience and trying another. In some observed cases, the entrepreneurs left unsatisfying jobs and endured long periods of unemployment, eventually finding opportunities to develop their own agencies.

The *independent* seeks autonomy and wants to avoid shared authority and decision making. His independence may derive from strong-mindedness about how things should be done or frustration from working under the control of others. The independent basically seeks to establish an organizational unit in which he is his own boss, free of direct internal interference or overwhelming external monitoring.

Various observed cases illustrate this orientation. For example, the headmaster of a private school left because of a conflict with his proprietor and established his own school. In another case, entrepreneurs left their posts in a state mental hospital to form their own children's agency. As noted earlier, Shapero also identifies the independent as an important entrepreneurial type.[25] Even more than the searchers, the independent is likely to moderate or restrict his entrepreneurial tendencies once he has achieved his goals of autonomy.

The *conserver*, a cousin of Downs's advocate and conserver and Maccoby's company man, is an organizational loyalist who carries out entrepreneurial activity (in the problem-response mode) only under circumstances (a crisis period) in which it is necessary to preserve the character and viability of his agency. The loyalty of the conserver derives from some combination of personal economic interest and cherished ideas, both of which have become embodied in, or associated with, the organization itself, through long-term affiliation and possibly even involvement with the founding of the institution. Like the independent and the searcher, the conserver is an occasional, sporadic entrepreneur when compared with the other, more chronically enterprising types. In one observed case, for example, a long-time employee who rose through the ranks of a large child-care agency helped to initiate a new program late in his career to alleviate public pressures and criticisms of his agency.

Power seekers derive satisfaction from climbing to the top, gaining recognition, and exerting influence over large groups of people and organizations. There are two kinds of power seekers—players and controllers.

Players like the chance their organization gives them to wield power and gain respect and acclaim within their organizations and in the world at large. Similar to Maccoby's gamesmen and jungle fighters and Downs's climbers, players are more willing to delegate authority than are controllers and hence they prefer larger organizations. In two observed cases, entrepreneurs expanded two of the largest social agencies and used this base to become prominent personalities in New York public affairs. As described by Meyer, Thomas Hoving would appear to be a preeminent player, combining political cunning with the skills and instincts of a showman.[26]

Controllers receive satisfaction directly from having authority over others and having the security of knowing what is going on under them. Such power seekers like to run tightly centrally controlled organizations and seek to expand those organizations so long as they can maintain the feeling of control. Some of the motivation of controllers may be understood by the observed tendency of many organizations to grow too large. As noted by Mueller:

> The case study literature of corporations is replete with situations in which the chief executives of a large diversified firm find themselves one day in a "crisis of control.". . . Frequently, these crises have been brewing for some time, but, owing to the lack of information about the division or individuals involved, the leaders of the firm are not aware that any problem exists until calamity strikes. What is more, these losses of control are not endemic solely to business corporations. The crises that have befallen large universities, branches of the government, the church and other large bureaucratic organizations in recent years are typically attributed to the lack of adequate information by those at the top of the difficulties being encountered by people further down the hierarchy."[27]

Controllers strongly wish to avoid such circumstances.

Income seekers are those entrepreneurs primarily driven by the motive of material self-aggrandizement in the form of income, future capital gain, and perquisites of office that substitute for personal expenditure. Various examples in the nursing-home industry are provided by Mendelson,[28] Vladeck,[29] and Grennon and Barsky.[30] Vladeck cites instances of wasteful spending, cheating, and corruption associated with Medicare and Medicaid financing, mostly in the proprietary sector. Mendelson also reviews instances in the nonprofit arena. Field studies reveal other cases with important elements of income seeking as an underlying drive. In extreme (maximizing) form, income seekers constitute the basic stereotype model of owners and managers implicit in the conventional theory of the firm in microeconomics.

The list of entrepreneurial characters is somewhat long, and there is some correlation and gradation of objectives from one type to another. The controller, for example, might be thought of as a hybrid of the independent and player types, the latter representing the power-seeking element and the former typifying the desire to retain control. Believers, poets, and professionals are similar to one another in their pursuit of concepts and ideas, albeit for different reasons and through different styles. Despite these similarities, however, the distinctions among the ten types and subtypes are useful for the development of the theory in the remainder of the book. The various kinds of entrepreneurs are summarized in table 5–1.

Entrepreneur Types and Venture Scenarios

There are certain correlations between the entrepreneurial stereotypes presented here and the venture scenarios described in chapter 4. Conservers, for example, would overwhelmingly associate themselves with the organizational problem-response mode of venture; searchers would tend to be active in the personal problem-response mode. Believers and poets lend themselves most readily to the intellectual or social flux of the initiative mode.

Other types of entrepreneurs are compatible with a wider range of scenarios. Professionals might prosper in the stability of the evolutionary situation or in the intellectual dynamism of the initiative mode. Architects would clearly engage their creative energies in the evolutionary mode, but might begin their venture agendas in the more open environment of the initiative mode or with the opportunities created by an organizational problem-response situation. Independents would also seize opportunities in the initiative or organizational problem-response circumstances.

Power seekers and income seekers are the most adaptable entrepreneurial types, willing to exploit ideas generated in the initiative-mode environment, create organizational environments for nurturing long-term projects in the evolutionary mode, or step into the adversity of a problem-response situation in order to create a turnaround that promises future power or wealth.

Table 5–1
Entrepreneurial Stereotype Models

Type	Principal Source of Satisfaction
Artist	
Architect	Pride in building and workmanship
Poet	Creativity and implementation of ideas
Professional	Acclaim of disciplinary peers
Believer	Pursuit of a cause or mission
Searcher	Self-identity
Independent	Autonomy
Conserver	Preservation of a cherished organization
Power seeker	
Controller	Stimulation and security of feeling in control of people
Player	Acclaim, notoriety, and excitement of having power
Income Seeker	Wealth

Because there is a rough correlation between the incidence of particular venture scenarios and the ambient conditions of an economic sector, the association of the various entrepreneurial types with specific scenarios means that those types will be differentially sensitive to their sectoral environments. Thus these environments will affect the degree to which entrepreneurs screened into a sector at one point in time later become active as agents of venture activity. The theory here will not make much of this point because the association between scenarios and ambient conditions is so rough and because it would unduly complicate matters. Nevertheless, the consideration of ambient conditions should be kept in mind as a qualifying element to the entrepreneur-based explanations of behaviors in specific contexts.

Risk

The entrepreneurial models are designed to capture the underlying drives that motivate the variety of individuals who are likely to become involved in significant entrepreneurial activity in industries that contain nonprofit agencies. The models also imply how much each of these types may be willing to take chances to achieve their basic goals. Therefore, a discussion of risk-taking behavior will help fill out the descriptions of these entrepreneurial characters.

Although financial and other risks of venture may be carried or shared by others, entrepreneurs are action-oriented people, often prone to putting themselves in precarious situations. All entrepreneurial activity, because it involves change, involves some risk, although often the risks associated with forbearing such activity may be just as severe. (In various observed cases ventures were required to avoid organizational collapse.) Risk-taking behavior varies by entrepreneurial type because there are different kinds of risk, each of which may be more or less important to each of the various types of entrepreneurs.

Entrepreneurs may incur risks along several dimensions in choosing to undertake, or not to undertake, ventures. The most common conception of risk is potential financial loss. Although this is a factor in many ventures, Williams and others argue that such risk is usually minimal in nonprofit activities.[31] As noted in chapter 3, financial risk is not necessarily overwhelming, even in the profit-oriented sector, nor is it necessarily the dominant mode of entrepreneurial risk taking. Vladeck for example argues that proprietary-nursing-home entrepreneurs have faced little financial risk, given a virtually assured flow of Medicaid patients and the failure of regulators to prevent them from diverting revenues from service quality to pay bills as they come due.[32]

Although entrepreneurs may not necessarily risk their own capital in ventures, some may risk job security or future income. Some observed ventures, for instance, were undertaken by newly installed executive directors who viewed the efficacy, if not the tenure, of their positions as dependent on their outcomes. In other cases, entrepreneurs sacrificed substantial levels of secure income in their efforts to establish ventures of highly uncertain prospect. Even a well-entrenched entrepreneuring executive may wonder if his job is at stake if a venture severely upsets the stability of his agency.

Perhaps an equally important personal dimension of risk is the legal jeopardy that entrepreneurs are sometimes willing to incur on behalf of their ventures. Entrepreneurs may take risks, sometimes defiantly, by opening programs before certifications or funds have been officially committed, circumventing regulations, or exposing themselves to other liabilities because of program exigencies.

Damage to professional reputation is another important source of entrepreneurial risk. Innovative ventures that run counter to professional thinking or that stir controversy can hurt the innovators if they fail. A variant of professional risk occurs when an entrepreneur who is a member of a corporate hierarchy (such as the Catholic church in several observed case studies) takes a legal or ideological position that conflicts with that of the establishment. Such a position risks rebuke by superiors and tarnishing of the entrepreneur's reputation. Professional reputation is also jeopardized when ventures threaten to upset the internal stability of an agency and hence bring the competence of the entrepreneur into question. Such risks are inherent, for example, in cases where human-service entrepreneurs bring program units for violent children onto their campuses or where an innovation such as an outpatient program in a residential institution upsets the organization's established structure, routine, or priorities.

Loss of managerial control is in itself a source of risk, making the entrepreneur's job more difficult and consuming. Such loss, in addition to its possible effects on job security and reputation, can lead to an overburden of personal responsibility as the entrepreneur attempts to deal with crises of instability and to reestablish an equilibrium. Perhaps more than economic losses or external judgments of program ineffectiveness, such loss of internal control may lead to a more direct sense of personal failure by the entrepreneur.

Personal overburden can be a serious source of risk to entrepreneurs, especially if ventures are expansive in nature or add significantly to the existing responsibilities of the entrepreneur. The same may be said of the personal sense of failure that some entrepreneurs seem to fear. Entrepreneurs who set high expectations for themselves and tend to feel personally responsible for their ventures find it difficult to live with negative outcomes. The egos of many entrepreneurs are tied up with their ventures.

To discern the risk-related behavior of the various entrepreneurial types, it is useful to distinguish between two concepts: risk consciousness and risk proneness. An entrepreneur is risk conscious if he seriously weighs particular elements of risk in his decision-making calculus. An entrepreneur is risk prone if he tends to take chances along particular dimensions of risk, consciously or not.

The artist is keenly risk conscious only with respect to the managerial environment of his agency. He is not especially sensitive to personal financial, job-security, legal, or professional risks and may therefore appear to be inadvertently risk prone in these areas. Whereas his ego is tied up with the success of his creations, he is willing to innovate and experiment with new forms without constraining himself to conservative strategies that might enable him to avoid failure. The artist is sensitive to his organizational environment, however, and makes decisions to prevent having that environment restrict his free hand. He will wish to avoid any new venture that threatens to tie him to administrative responsibilities and will seek to incorporate the delegation of responsibility into the design of new ventures. The artist may seize opportunities to increase his flexibility or the creative resources at his command, and this will sometimes involve calculated risk taking, balancing the potential administrative burdens against the potential new opportunities. The latter dilemma is most serious for the poet-type artist. The architectural type may view administrative tinkering as part of his own creative realm, deriving direct satisfaction from toying with and perfecting new (perhaps larger and more complex) administrative mechanisms.

The professional will be most conscious of risks in the legal, managerial, and professional-reputation dimensions. He may also be conscious of risks to job security and of financial (income) loss to the extent that professional standing may be influenced by economic status or rank. In general, the professional tends to be conservative on ventures that involve potential organizational instability, legal jeopardy, or job security, fearing that incidents could hurt his reputation. On the other hand, professionals may be inadvertently risk prone with respect to overburdens of personal responsibility, perhaps taking on more than they can easily handle, because of the potential professional accolades. The most interesting risk-related problem of the professional is to weigh the undertaking of controversial ventures whose success can substantially enhance professional standing but whose failure can seriously damage that standing. In such cases, the professional will take a calculated risk, weighing the potential losses to reputation from managerial and legal problems, loss of job security, or ridicule of an idea turned sour against the potential recognition gained from championing a new concept.

The believer is the most risk prone of all entrepreneurial types, putting the implementation of his cherished ideas, or progress in his cause, above all else. Minimizing personal ramifications, he tends to be risk prone with respect to financial security, legal jeopardy, professional reputation, and administrative overburden. He may even put a positive value on creating instability (managerial or otherwise) in the belief that this is the most effective road to reform. Such a rationale appears to have characterized James Dixon, former president and innovator of Antioch College: "Dixon clings to a perverse form of courage, believing that only thin ice is worth skating on. . . . "[33] Dixon is quoted as saying that "(Antioch) has no obligation to pursue its own survival as an end," clearly an unusual, risk-oriented stance for an administrator, but one apparently deriving from a strong sense of social mission.

Believers may be forced to take calculated risks if the efficacy of the cause or the potential of the entrepreneur in working toward that cause are uncertain. Thus a venture that might substantially advance the cause if it worked but that might damage the movement or the entrepreneur's role in it if it failed would cause some hesitation. Ralph Nader would have to think carefully about a project designed to expose the hazards of coal power, for example. Such a project might result in a considerable boost for the use of nonpolluting, renewable energy sources, but it might also strengthen the hand of nuclear-power interests, and thus damage the position of clean-power advocates.

The searcher is by definition a potential entrepreneur without a well-established organizational or professional base, although he may have some disciplinary training and a current job that provides income. Risks to managerial stability and personal administrative overburden are thus irrelevant to him. On the other hand, the searcher appears to be risk prone with respect to financial loss, job security, and professional reputation because he is willing to range far and wide for a long period of time and with great sacrifice to find his niche in the professional or business world. He is willing to leave his present employment and pass up substantial income to consider a wide variety of venture (and other employment) opportunities, even those outside his disciplinary training or realm of work experience, before settling on a course of action. The most serious problem for the searcher is to choose a venture that will suit his personal needs—one that will give him a renewed sense of purpose and self-worth but that will not overwhelm his capabilities and bring about further frustration or uneasiness.

The independent is an entrepreneur who knows what he wants to do (managerially and professionally) and wants to be free to do it without the constraints of sharing authority with others. He may or may not have secure employment prior to his venture, but if he does he may risk it to break free. At that stage, therefore, the independent is risk prone with respect to financial loss, job security, personal overburden, legal liability, and even professional reputation, although his personal professional ideas and desire for managerial discretion may be the very source of his quest for autonomy. Having succeeded in setting up his own organization, however, the independent is likely to become risk averse. His main goal will be to preserve his autonomy and run his business as he likes. He may cease to become an entrepreneur at all, in the sense of sponsoring future ventures. If he does continue, he is most likely to resemble the conserver.

As his name implies, the conserver is a basically risk-averse personality who is seriously concerned with job security and avoiding activities that threaten legal jeopardy, internal instability, or loss of reputation for the organization. The conserver does not become an entrepreneur until the organization, or his position in it, is troubled and a venture promises to rescue it. He will then move into action, taking calculated risks of the legal, professional, and managerial varieties against the potential for successful resurrection.

Power seekers are the most flamboyant risk takers of all entrepreneurs, although their risk taking is usually calculated. They will gamble with their own financial well-being, job security, and professional reputation and will risk legal problems and organizational instabilities, but only if there is reasonable hope for a substantial payoff in terms of increased personal power or if implementation of the venture is in itself an exercise in power playing. Controller-type power seekers will be substantially more conservative than players with respect to potential managerial instability because they derive their satisfaction not only from manipulating but from feeling they are in control. In contrast, players will present a bolder front to the outside world to suit their larger ego needs. However, their risk taking is held in check by those same ego needs, namely the desire to avoid personal failure. Both controller and player varieties of power seekers are prone to personal administrative overburden—the controller because he constantly seeks to increase surveillance of his operation, and the player because he tends to increase his organizational domain over time.

The income seeker is perhaps the most calculating of risk takers, weighing the financial implications (benefits and costs) of each venture decision carefully. He will also be mindful of legal and managerial risks insofar as they might put his organization's economic position in jeopardy. The income seeker may be indifferent to professional reputation and inadvertently risk prone in this area, although regulatory mechanisms may force him to translate professional standards and norms into dollars and cents. As Vladeck observes for nursing homes, even the greediest operator has to show some minimal concern for image, the safety of his investment, and personal legal liability.[34] A young income seeker is also prone to a risk of personal overburden, hustling to find financial backers and accumulate working capital or to establish a foothold on the rungs of a corporate ladder.

Older income seekers may have accumulated enough capital to live their lives with more moderation.

Notes

1. Joseph A. Schumpeter, *The Theory of Economic Development* (Cambridge: Harvard University Press, 1949).

2. David C. McClelland, "The Two Faces of Power," chapter 19 in *Human Motivation*, eds. David C. McClelland and Robert S. Steele (Morris, N.J.: General Learning Press, 1973).

3. Richard C. Cornuelle, *Reclaiming the American Dream* (Westminster, Md: Random House, 1965).

4. Victor H. Vroom, *Work and Motivation* (New York: John Wiley, 1964).

5. James Q. Wilson, *Political Organizations* (New York: Basic Books, 1973).

6. David G. Winter, "The Need for Power," Chapter 17 in *Human Motivation*, eds. David C. McClelland and Robert S. Steele (Morris, N.J.: General Learning Press, 1973).

7. David C. McClelland and Robert I. Watson Jr., "Power Motivation and Risk-Taking Behavior," Chapter 11 in *Human Motivation*, eds. David C. McClelland and Robert S. Steele, (Morris, N.J.: General Learning Press, 1973).

8. Albert Shapero, "Some Social Dimensions of Entrepreneurship" (Draft, Ohio State University, presented to Conference on Entrepreneurship Research, Baylor University, March 1980).

9. Michael Maccoby, *The Gamesman* (New York: Simon and Schuster, 1976).

10. Anthony Downs, *Inside Bureaucracy* (Boston: Little, Brown and Company, 1967).

11. William Niskanen, *Bureaucracy and Representative Government* (Chicago: Aldine-Atherton, 1971).

12. Oliver E. Williamson, *The Economics of Discretionary Behavior* (Chicago: Markham, 1967).

13. Ibid.

14. Herbert Simon, *Administrative Behavior* (New York: Free Press, 1965).

15. Richard M. Cyert and James G. March, *A Behavioral Theory of the Firm* (Englewood Cliffs, N.J.: Prentice-Hall, 1963).

16. Roger B. Parks and Elinor Ostrom, "Towards a Model of the Effect of Inter- and Intraorganizational Structure on Public Bureau Service Out-

puts," (Paper No. T–80, Workshop in Political Theory and Policy Analysis, Indiana University, March 1980).

17. Private communication with Richard R. Nelson. See also Israel M. Kirzner, *Perception, Opportunity, and Profit* (Chicago: University of Chicago Press, 1979).

18. Edith Evans Ashbury, "Angus L. Bowmer, 74, Founder of Oregon Shakespeare Festival," *New York Times*, May 29, 1979.

19. Waldemar A. Nielsen, *The Endangered Sector* (New York: Columbia University Press, 1979).

20. Bruce C. Vladeck, *Unloving Care* (New York: Basic Books, 1980).

21. Cornuelle, *American Dream.*

22. Woflgang Saxon, "Thomas Kielty Scherman Dies; Founded Little Orchestra Society," *New York Times*, May 5, 1979.

23. Joel F. Handler, Betsy Ginsberg, and Arthur Snow, "The Public Interest Law Industry," in *Public Interest Law,* eds. Burton Weisbrod, Joel F. Handler, and Neil Komesar (Berkeley: University of California Press, 1978).

24. Shapero, "Dimensions of Entrepreneurship."

25. Ibid.

26. Karl E. Meyer, *The Art Museum* (New York: William Morrow and Company, 1979).

27. Dennis C. Mueller, "A Life Cycle Theory of the Firm," *Journal of Industrial Economics* 20 (July 1972):3.

28. Mary A. Mendelson, *Tender Loving Greed* (New York: Alfred A. Knopf, 1974).

29. Vladeck, *Unloving Care.*

30. Jacqueline Grennon and Robert Barsky, "Case Studies in Nursing Home Entrepreneurship" PONPO working paper 20 (Institution for Social and Policy Studies, Yale University, 1980).

31. Harold S. Williams, "Entrepreneurs in the Non-Profit World," *In Business,* July–August 1980.

32. Vladeck, *Unloving Care.*

33. Gerald Grant, "A Network of Antiochs," in *Academic Transformation*, eds. David Riesman and Verne A. Stadtman (New York: McGraw Hill, 1973).

34. Vladeck, *Unloving Care.*

6 Screening by Industry

Discussion so far has focused on certain universal qualities of entrepreneurship in the economy, that is, on motivations and circumstances of enterprising found in virtually every formally organized field of social and economic activity. This chapter will begin to distinguish among qualities of entrepreneurship found in different parts of the economy by differentiating entrepreneurship according to industry or field of activity, for example, health care, child care, education, the arts, and so on. Chapter 7 will further distinguish enterprising behavior by economic sector—profit making, nonprofit, and public—within industries.

To differentiate entrepreneurship by industry it is necessary to delineate structural characteristics of fields that differentially attract (or repel) the various types of entrepreneurs and then to determine how these characteristics tend to screen *potential* entrepreneurial populations into different parts of the economy, thereby affecting the distribution of entrepreneurial motivations within any given industry. The emphasis on the term *potential* is important. I shall argue that entrepreneurs ultimately active in a given field may not become immediately mobilized, either because they may take time to mature and gain the requisite knowledge or because sectoral conditions (as delineated in chapter 4) are not immediately appropriate or attractive for venture. Nonetheless, the screening process creates pools of latent entrepreneurial talent that differ by industry in their motivational content and hence in their ultimate behavior.

I shall argue that the relevant structural characteristics of industries that screen the populations of potential entrepreneurs include the following.

1. The intrinsic character of the service itself, in particular, whether it is basically a social or a technical service, whether it involves an altruistic objective, and whether it stresses creativity. In brief, this theory will state that entrepreneurs tend to be drawn from academic disciplines associated with particular industries and that those disciplines will tend to attract personnel with motivations appropriate to the service at issue. Hence, to a strong degree, screening by discipline also serves as screening by industry for entrepreneurship.

2. The degree to which the field is dominated or controlled by one or more of the organized professions. This factor will be seen to influence the degree to which entrepreneurship can come from outside the ranks of

dominant disciplines or from the ranks of alternative (coexisting) disciplines.

3. The degree of concentration of the field, that is, the degree of dominance by a few organizations and the ease of entry by new firms or agencies. This factor will be seen to especially influence the career choices of latent entrepreneurs who are concerned with power, independence, and opportunities to pursue individual ideas and beliefs.

4. The social significance or priority attached by society to a given field. This again will be seen to influence the career choices of certain latent entrepreneurs whose interests focus on power and material gain.

The mechanics of entrepreneurial selection among industries may involve three alternative (complementary) processes or trajectories by which individuals enter the latent entrepreneurial pool.

1. Individuals make early choices of disciplinary training and career tracks that logically channel into particular industries. Such individuals pursue their careers in these industries and at some point become mobilized as entrepreneurs. For example, trained social workers enter social-service career ladders in agencies, and some eventually become entrepreneurs. Thus, disciplines attached to fields become a common source of entrepreneurial talent. This is perhaps the most common entrepreneurial trajectory in service industries, but is more heavily followed by professionals, conservers, and believers than other types of entrepreneurs.

2. Individuals make career changes later in life, after having gained various work and educational experiences. Such career shifts are inhibited by intrafield requirements for disciplinary training, but in industries in which these requirements are flexible, such as therapeutic-camping or services to violent or severely handicapped children, the pool of latent entrepreneurial talent will include membership from a variety of loosely related disciplines (education, social work, and psychology). This route tends to be characteristic of the searcher, but is not unusual for other flexible or wide-ranging types, such as artists, power seekers, and income seekers.

3. Individuals make purposeful, managerially oriented choices of generalist disciplines, such as business administration or law, that can provide them with continued flexibility in choice of industry. Alternatively, individuals with other types of disciplinary training or even without much formal training pursue managerial experiences early in their careers in organizations in a variety of industries. Often such trajectories only delay field specialization and a long-term choice of industry. Indeed Thurow observes, for the profit sector, that most entrepreneurial and managerial personnel do tend to become specialized in a given industry:

> If we ask why managers with large internal savings do not start subsidiaries
> in high profit industries rather than reinvesting in their own low profit

industries, we come face to face with the entire structure of restricted competition in the U.S. economy. Barriers to entry are often high, and managers often do not have the specialized knowledge necessary to make profits in another industry. The existence of high profits in the cosmetics industry, for example, does not mean that iron and steel executives could earn high profits there.[1]

In some cases, however, the (latent) entrepreneur does manage to maintain his flexibility as a long-term career pattern. Hence in industries such as the nursing-home industry that permit easy entry and reward administrative skill or financial management as important specialities, the pool of potential entrepreneurial talent is expanded to include this group of entrepreneurial generalists (see Vladeck).[2] This route tends to be more characteristic of power seekers, income seekers, and some architects than of other entrepreneur types.

Given these various career-sorting processes, the character of the resulting pool of potential entrepreneurs available to a given industry will depend on the particular structural characteristics of that industry. These characteristics are discussed below.

Nature of the Service. Services can be characterized as having various degrees of social involvement, technical sophistication, and requirements for creativity. The social services, for example, rank high on the first of these dimensions, as they strongly involve activities directly addressed to helping the less fortunate and improving social conditions. Higher education would score somewhat lower on direct social involvement but higher on technical sophistication, that is, demands for technical excellence, than social service. Health services would rank high on technical sophistication because they require intensive training, scientific discipline, and meticulous operational skills, and they would rank lower than social or educational services in the social-involvement dimension. Scientific research would be generally more demanding of technical sophistication, moderately demanding of creativity, and low in direct social involvement. The arts would obviously stress creativity as well as technical sophistication.

These dimensions of service character affect the screening of latent entrepreneurs primarily through processes 1 and 2 described above by differentially appealing to the principal motivations represented by each of the postulated entrepreneurial stereotypes. For example, latent believers will be drawn to fields involving high levels of social involvement, where causes are clear and easy to articulate and where crusading is an accepted form of behavior. Searchers, who may actively be engaged in process 2 during their entrepreneurial phase, may also find fields of social involvement appealing because they might find relevance and meaning for themselves in the work being done for society or in the direct human relationships entailed by these fields. Conservers will also be disproportionately drawn to such fields because organizations with cherished traditions of service are more likely to develop in such contexts. Institutions like the settlement house provide examples of this phenomenon.

Fields characterized by high levels of technical sophistication are generally the domain of the professional (although not all fields with high levels of professionalism are technical). These fields favor rational discourse, methodological standards, and scientific patience and scrutiny. Believers may operate in technical fields, espousing strongly held theories and methods, but they need to cloak these beliefs in the form of rationally derived proposals. Many ventures in the medical and psychological service areas illustrate the professional entrepreneurial character in technical disciplines.

Technically sophisticated fields may also be attractive to potential entrepreneurs of the architectural variety. Sophisticated technologies—in engineering, research, or the health fields, for example—can provide participants with the means to create new structures, products, and services. In hospitals, for example, generous reimbursement formulas have financed the development of sophisticated laboratories and treatment units founded on the latest scientific technologies.[3] Thus new medical advances or computer-research technologies may become the basis for building up and reorganizing entire organizational structures, for example, specialized-care units in hospitals, management-information systems, and research centers in universities.

Finally, fields that emphasize creativity are more likely to attract the latent artist, especially the poet. Traditionally, artistically trained individuals have been the primary management and entrepreneurial source for museums, theaters, and musical and dance enterprises (consistent with process 1). In museums, for instance, directors are heavily drawn from those with graduate degrees in fine arts.[4] Only recently has there developed a tendency to consider the need for managerial skills. (For example, see McQuade.)[5] The same creative, expressionistic urges that underlie performance and achievement in artistic fields are thus likely to motivate and underwrite entrepreneurial enterprise via projects that strike out in original directions and bear messages of philosophic meaning or emotional content.

Professional Control. The degree to which organized professions control employment and maintain fundamental authority and power within a given industry affects the pool of entrepreneurial talent available to that field in three ways. First, disciplinary control tends to institutionalize the nature of the service as described above and to protect it from corruption by extra-disciplinary influences (such as the influences of commercialism or the perspectives of other disciplines). Thus the professions reemphasize the labeling of services as technical, helping, or creative undertakings. In part, therefore, social work is a helping profession, with its implications for self-sacrifice and public service, by definition of the profession as well as the inherent character of the work. Hence those who would enter without this perspective (via process 1) are discouraged from doing so. Similarly, medicine or law are defined as technical professions, thereby limiting entry of those with other, less rigorous points of view. Nielson observes, for example, that "the AMA battled unrelentingly against the licensing of osteopaths, chiropractors, and optometrists."[6] Finally, the arts require a creative, expressionistic viewpoint in a vein parallel to the alternative orientations taken by helping and technical professions. Overall, therefore, the result of professional control is to screen even more strongly—believers and conservers into the helping fields, professionals into the technical fields, and artists into the creative fields.

The second effect of professional control of an industry is to limit the processes through which the pool of entrepreneurial talent is formed. Disciplines require unique modes of training that must normally be undertaken at the beginning of a career. Thus process 1 is the most viable mode of entry; career-switch (2) and generalist (3) modes become more unlikely as disciplinary control becomes tighter. The education, legal, and medical fields all provide relatively stringent examples. One result is to substantially reduce the chance that searchers will be part of the entrepreneurial pool or that generalists of any type (that is, those who would enter through scenario 3) can infiltrate a specialized industry.

A third important way in which professional control influences the formation of the latent entrepreneurial pool is through the inculcation of ethical values. The aforementioned altruism of the helping professions, the emphasis on intellectual honesty and technical competence of the technical disciplines, and the elevation of artistic expression by the creative professions, constitute only part of this value structure. Professions also have different values with respect to money-making, achievement of power, and autonomy (solo practice versus teamwork). The helping professions, because of their self-sacrifice ethic, tend to deemphasize wealth and, to a lesser degree, power accumulation, thus discouraging income seekers and power seekers. Technical professions tend to encourage income augmentation as a virtue, signifying societal recognition of their importance, competence, and special skills and investments in advanced training and education, although they will also express disdain for irresponsible money seekers. The creative fields are relatively neutral in these domains, neither recognizing money and power as symbols of status, nor disdaining them as sins, except to discourage power seeking or income seeking at the sacrifice of originality or artistic achievement. Often, however, the emphasis on the intrinsic value of the work leads to a relative deemphasis of material reward.

For example, McQuade[7] and Meyer[8] both allude to the low pay and economic insecurity of museum directors. According to Meyer:

> There are few professions in the United States that offer more modest economic rewards to those holding graduate degrees than does the museum calling. Because museum work is thought to be pleasant, prestigious, and even glamorous, museum professionals are expected to settle for working for relatively low wages.

Similar observations apply to other areas of artistic endeavor.

In practice, of course, industries are controlled by discipline-oriented professions in varying degrees. Although professions do tend to seek exclusive control over particular industries, the degrees of dominance achieved vary considerably from field to field. This variation reflects, in part, the maturity of an industry and its degree of evolution from a wide-open, turbulent field of activity to a more stable industrial regime (see chapter 4).

There are three qualitatively different cases of professional dominance.

1. In some industries, such as health care, certain arts, or higher education, disciplinary control tends to be essentially complete. Significant participation at the staff level and ultimate managerial control in these areas is virtually precluded to those without a medical degree, artistic credentials, or advanced graduate training in an academic discipline.

2. In other fields, such as residential care of children, fragmentation occurs, with different disciplines claiming similar domains of service under different labels. Thus social workers, psychologists, and educators may all be involved in sheltering emotionally disturbed children, with similar services provided under the names of residential school, foster-care agency, and residential-treatment center.

3. In still other fields, such as nursing-home care for the elderly or day care for children, participation and managerial control are much less restricted by discipline and hence are open to people with a wide variety of backgrounds, including those without special training for providing the services of interest.[9]

Clearly, fields of the first variety will confine the entrepreneurial pool heavily to those trained in the discipline (via scenario 1) and hence to those entrepreneurial types encouraged or selected by that discipline. Industries of the second variety will add diversity to the pool by mixing the flows from alternative disciplines. Industries of the third kind will draw on an even wider entrepreneurial pool, with participation from a variety of disciplines, including generalists and field switchers who enter through processes 2 and 3.

In no case does the disciplinary filter work perfectly. First, no industry can be described as a completely closed professional shop. In medicine, mavericks (osteopaths, chiropractors, optometrists) do manage to operate outside the medical establishment. Within the established boundaries of industries tightly controlled by a single discipline and heavily imbued with a particular work and moral ethic, individuals with motivations that deviate from that ethic will slip through, either because their values can change after they have become educated in the discipline and gained some experience or because they see through the disciplinary screen to a set of opportunities for pursuing alternative motivations. Still, an important sorting of motivations occurs by industry, not only because of inherent service character but also because of the degree of organized disciplinary control.

Industry Structure. Industries vary in the degree to which they are dominated by a few large organizations. In the commercial and industrial sectors, monopolization has long been a key concern of public policy and the focus of antitrust legislation. In industries in which the nonprofit and public sectors participate (perhaps alongside proprietary activity), the concentration of activity also varies significantly, although the issues of competition and collusion are often considered less important, if not irrelevant (see below). Some fields, such as day care, nursing-home care, or residential child care, are characterized by the presence of many relatively small producing organizations, none of which represents a significant proportion of the total activity of the industry within a given community. In other areas, teaching hospitals or opera companies, for example, providers are relatively few, and activity is more concentrated in the hands of a small number of organizations. In general, the presence of scale economies in production helps account for monopolistic or oligopolistic organization in the goods-producing sectors of the economy. In the service sector, where nonprofits are concentrated, such economies tend to be less important. Still, there may be significant variation among service industries in this characteristic, which may help account for some of the variation in the concentration of activity across fields. Moreover, concentration may also reflect the age of an industry, if economic pressures or other considerations have led small, young agencies to merge or consolidate over time. Industry structure thus proxies some of the evolutionary factors that underlie venture activity, discussed in chapter 4.

Related to the question of concentration is the ease of entry into a given industry by new agencies or organizations. Activity concentrated in a few organizations may reflect relatively large capital requirements for operation, which represents a barrier to new entry. Furthermore, concentration is likely to be accompanied by governmental planning controls that attempt to ensure that facilities are efficiently utilized and meet suitable standards. Thus government may restrict the entry of new hospitals, nursing homes, day-care centers, or foster-care agencies to those which meet prespecified quality, safety, architectural, financial, and administrative standards and can demonstrate need for their services and ensure that they will not simply dilute the enrollments of existing agencies. Comprehensive planning and regulation date back to the mid 1960s in the hospital field and, have recently come into their own in the nursing-home industry. (See Lehman,[10] Vladeck,[11] and Dunlop[12] for review of developments in these areas.) Vladeck, for example, documents the relationship between entry regulation and industry concentration. Newer and smaller firms are denied entry (or driven out) by the costs of administrative procedures and capital requirements imposed by regulatory agencies.

A rough correlation between industry structure and the distribution of industrial activity among profit-making, nonprofit, and public sectors is observed here. Within the service fields in which nonprofits participate, economic activity tends to become more concentrated within fewer, larger organizations as one moves from the profit-making, to nonprofit, to governmental form. For example, in 1976, for-profit hospitals averaged 98.3 beds, compared with 195 for nonprofit, 119 for local-government, and 611 for state-government hospitals.[13] For nursing homes in 1973, Dunlop documents average sizes of 69, 85, and 110 beds for proprietary, nonprofit, and governmental institutions respectively.[14] For elementary schools in 1976, enrollment figures were 422 public versus 218 nonpublic; for secondary schools, 573 public versus 324 nonpublic; and for higher education, 6,317 public versus 1,423 nonpublic.[15]

For museums, size measurement is complicated by difficulties in reconciling estimates of full-time, part-time, and volunteer staff with institutional definitions. In terms of operating budgets for 1971–1972, private nonprofits slightly outnumbered public museums in the category under $100,000, whereas the reverse was true for the $100,000–$250,000 category. Equal representation was found in the category over $250,000. In the special category of museums attached to educational institutions, a sharp differential existed between larger public and smaller private museums.[16] In day care of young children in 1976–1977, the Abt study found that among day-care centers not enrolling publicly subsidized children, the profit centers averaged an enrollment of 43 children, compared with 55 for nonprofit (including governmental).[17] For centers enrolling publicly subsidized children, the figures were 49 versus 51.

Governments tend to locate most of their activity related to a particular function (such as child welfare or health) within a single hierarchical structure or in large divisions of such a structure, for example, in departments of health and major public clinics. In contrast, proprietary services are generally not the focus of a large corporation but are more the domain of the small, independent operator—the doctor, the educator, or the consultant who is in business for himself or with a partner or small company. Nonprofits, because they often entail community-wide sponsorship, are frequently required by government or other sponsors to meet various standards of administration and service output and, perhaps because they are subject to less stringent antitrust controls than are profit makers,[18] they tend to represent a middle ground—larger and more bureaucratic than proprietaries, but smaller and more fragmented than governmental units. The distinctions among sectors will be elaborated further in the next chapter. At this point, it will suffice to note that industry concentration is correlated with the distribution of industry activity across sectors, increasing as emphasis moves from proprietary, to nonprofit, to government provision. Thus screening of entrepreneurs by industry, because of concentration effects, will tend to occur in tandem with some of the sectoral-screening effects considered in chapter 7.

The effect of industry concentration is simply to make particular industries more or less attractive to particular entrepreneurial characters. Thus when potential entrepreneurs make career choices they are assumed to have some appreciation of the current (and likely future) structure of the industries that they select or reject. Several types of potential entrepreneurs will be influenced by industry concentration and ease of entry.

Independents will prefer industries that are relatively unconcentrated, in which small organizations are common and new entry is relatively easy. The ultimate objective of such an entrepreneur will be to try to establish his own new organization or to gain the helm of an existing agency within a reasonably short period of time.

Searchers may begin their careers in concentrated fields in which they may become overwhelmed or frustrated by large organizations that impose fixed career ladders and burdensome controls on employees. Ultimately, however, they move to industries in which new entry is possible or in which many different agencies exist that may be explored for their career potentials.

Power seekers will prefer concentrated fields that feature large organizations, where opportunities abound for assuming responsibility over large groups of people. Player-type power seekers will prefer larger organizations (and hence more concentrated fields) than controller-type power seekers, because the latter fear loss of effective control as the organization grows. Players, on the other hand, benefit from the grander platforms and greater notoriety provided by bigger organizations.

Conservers will prefer fields of modest concentration that feature organizations large, stable, and mature enough to have established traditions and provide a sense of economic security but that are not so large as to have become impersonal and institutional or mechanical in character.

Professionals will tend to select industries that are moderately to highly concentrated and provide adequate resource bases for pursuit of their disciplinary endeavors. Professionals may seek to avoid highly concentrated industries, however, if they perceive the large organizations within those fields to be inimical to the flexibility required for professional development. Professionals will also avoid industries that are so fragmented as to offer little promise of resource aggregation sufficient to support state-of-the-art activity and methodological advances.

Artists will select industries that exhibit a moderate to low concentration of activity. The architectural variety of artist will seek organizations large enough to provide a resource base sufficient to support his penchant for building and program development, yet small enough so that new enterprises are both noticeable and identifiable as one's own product. Artists of the poet variety generally desire less concentration than architectural types; they prefer to remain unencumbered by administrative responsibilities and constraints and free to explore a variety of ideas. The poet may thus have stronger feelings about ease of entry than the architect, because he may feel less bound to remain with particular organizations for long periods of time (see chapter 9). Both types of artist enjoy nurturing projects from scratch, but the architect prefers a sector that will ultimately support programs of significant size, whereas the poet is generally more comfortable with smallness and flexibility.

The Income Seeker has no strict preferences regarding the concentration of activity, size of organizations, or entry possibilities in a given field. Unconcentrated fields can present income opportunities through investment in the formation or building up of small enterprises, whereas concentrated fields may present opportunities for internal advancement in large agencies, matched by salary and benefit increases. As Vladeck observes, however, the former scenario often seems more compelling, because money can be made quickly in rapidly growing fields not yet dominated by a few large firms.[19] Having entered a weakly concentrated field, the income seeker will work toward its concentration as a long-term strategy to increase income, or he will leave once his fortune is made and opportunities have diminished.

Social Priority. Through the expression of economic demands and the allocation of resources as well as the more elusive concept of prestige, society tends to attach greater importance and social status to some fields than to others. For example, among industries in which nonprofits typically participate, health and scientific research tend to be elevated (in the United States, at least) and education and social service hold more precarious positions in the public's mind and in the economy. Social priorities will, of course, vary over time, reflecting demographic trends, technological change, cycles of economic prosperity, and other factors that contribute to the ambient conditions for an industry's development. For theoretical purposes, however, it is assumed that potential entrepreneurs are able to make reasoned, fixed judgments on what these priorities are likely to be for the future.

Accordingly, the relative status of industries is assumed to influence career choices and hence the pools of latent entrepreneurial talent that become available to particular industries. (Sometimes the effect of social priorities on career choice is made quite explicit through public policy, as when the government invests in the training of scientists and engineers as the United States did in the late 1950s and early 1960s, or in physicians, as in the 1960s.)

Differences in social priority among industries will have the strongest effects on two entrepreneurial types—the income seeker and the power seeker. Income seekers will look toward rich or expanding fields as presenting the strongest opportunities for material reward. Power seekers, especially those of the player variety, will see such industries as the locus of where the action is. There they will seek the most notable platforms for achieving fame and influence over the largest and most important sets of people and resources.

Other entrepreneurial types may also be influenced in their career choices by the social status of alternative industries, albeit to lesser degrees. Professionals and artists may see the more prestigious fields as providing stronger resource bases on which to pursue the kinds of intellectual or creative stimulation they value. Alternatively, searchers may see fields of emerging social interest as new, uncrowded, vistas to explore in their efforts to find satisfying careers.

Independents and believers will be relatively indifferent to the social priority attached to alternative industries. The independent essentially seeks autonomy and may even tend to avoid fields that are in the spotlight, preferring environments in which he is more likely to be left alone. The believer is somewhat similar in this respect. Although industries of greater social priority may provide a wide set of opportunities for taking up social causes or sponsoring particular policies, the believer is more likely to attach himself to causes or fields that he feels are underserved and require new attention by society.

Perspective. The discussion in this chapter is based on the idea that pools of latent entrepreneurial talent available for enterprise within particular industries are determined by people's choices of disciplines and careers, usually made early in their working lives. Furthermore, this chapter postulates that such career choices are influenced by aspirants' perceptions of the character of industries associated with their disciplinary training and career paths.

Finally, some consistency is assumed between the motivations of people at the stage of career choice and the motivations that they exhibit when they become entrepreneurs.

These assumptions require some further explanation and elaboration. First, there is usually a significant delay between time of career choice and time of entrepreneurial activity. Thus potential entrepreneurs are assumed to exhibit a certain amount of foresight as to the future character of industries. In particular, except for fields in which the entrepreneurial talent pool is formed significantly through field-switching (2) or generalist (3) modes, the latent entrepreneur is assumed to make reasonable guesses as to the future character of industries, manifested by disciplinary choices.

Second, this chapter has focused on motivations as a prime selection variable for sorting latent entrepreneurial types into alternative careers and industries. Chance and inherent individual talents are also involved in this process. Random deviations are assumed to obtain across industries but not bias the postulated selection processes in any particular direction.

Talent raises more troubling questions. Certainly the screening process that tracks individuals into disciplines hinges heavily on skills (talent) as a prime discriminating factor. Tone-deaf people will not be channeled into musical careers nor will those with limited mathematical abilities be channeled into computer programming. Perhaps more to the point, industries that require certain relatively rare talents will strongly attract those with the requisite potential.

On this basis one might even argue that individuals with high potential for entrepreneurial skills—organizing, salesmanship, leadership and charisma, and a good business sense—would be strongly attracted to commercial areas that positively and explicitly reward and encourage such skills. Williams suggests this situation,[20] and Cornuelle observes that:

> competitive pressure has developed in the commercial sector a breed of gifted promoters and organizers of commercial action. We need to create such a breed in the independent [nonprofit] sector. They are our scarcest resource.[21]

In relative terms, such claims of entrepreneurial steering toward the commercial sector may be correct. Nonetheless, as illustrated in chapter 3, entrepreneurial talent is found in noticeable quantities in many industries in which entrepreneurship is not a particularly enshrined concept.

Thus substantive individual interests and motivations, perhaps more than innate skills, heavily influence career tracks. Furthermore, there is an obvious, inseparable correlation between what one enjoys and what one is able to do well. Skills and motivations are thus likely to go hand in hand.

This chapter has taken the perspective that the composition of the pool of potential entrepreneurial talent is influenced by processes of career and discipline choice. It argues further that choice of discipline and career orientation is itself influenced not only by chance and talent, but more by a positive, if not self-conscious, matching of latent entrepreneurial motives to the character of industries to which given types of disciplinary training or early work experience ultimately apply. Four relevant industry characteristics were identified: the nature of the service, that is, its social, technical, or creative orientation; the pattern of professional or disciplinary control over the industry; the size of organizations, degree of industry concentration, and ease of entry; and the social priority attached to the industry as a whole. These characteristics act as indicators or signals used by the various distinct entrepreneurial types to sort themselves among industries.

It is important to recognize that particular industries, for example, hospitals or higher education, must be described as clusters, or packages, of characteristics along these four dimensions. The four unidimensional analyses of sorting by entrepreneurial type must be combined to arrive at specific conclusions about the motivational distribution of entrepreneurship for any particular industry. Furthermore, these clusters exhibit substantial intra-industry variation, arising in good measure from sectoral divisions within industries. Screening by sector is the subject of the next chapter.

Notes

1. Lester Thurow, *The Zero Sum Society* (New York: Basic Books, 1980).

2. Bruce C. Vladeck, *Unloving Care* (New York: Basic Books, 1980).

3. Ibid.

4. *Museums U.S.A.: A Survey Report* (National Research Center of the Arts for the National Endowment for the Arts, Washington, D.C. 1974).

5. Walter McQuade, "Management Problems Enter the Picture at Art Museums," *Fortune*, July 1974.

6. Waldemar A. Nielson, *The Endangered Sector* (New York: Columbia University Press, 1979).

7. McQuade, "Management Problems."

8. Karl E. Meyer, *The Art Museum* (New York: William Morrow and Co., 1979).

9. Jacqueline Grennon and Robert Barsky, "An Exploration of Entrepreneurship in the Field of Nursing Home Care for the Elderly" (PONPO working paper 20, Institution for Social and Policy Studies, Yale University, 1980).

10. Edward W. Lehman, *Coordinating Health Care* (Beverly Hills: Sage Publications, 1975).

11. Vladeck, *Unloving Care*.

12. Burton Dunlop, *The Growth of Nursing Home Care* (Lexington, Mass.: Lexington Books, D.C. Heath and Company, 1979).

13. *Statistical Abstract of the United States, 1978*, U.S. Department of Commerce, Bureau of the Census.

14. Dunlop, *Nursing Home Care*.

15. *Statistical Abstract*.

16. *Museums U.S.A.*

17. Craig Coelen, Frederic Glantz, and Daniel Calore, *Day Care Centers in the U.S.: A National Profile 1976–1977* (Cambridge: Abt Books, 1979).

18. Henry B. Hansmann, "The Role of Nonprofit Enterprise," *Yale Law Journal*, April 1980.

19. Vladeck, *Unloving Care*.

20. Harold S. Williams, "Entrepreneurs in the Nonprofit World," *In Business*, July–August 1980.

21. Richard C. Cornuelle, *Reclaiming the American Dream* (Westminster, Md: Random House, 1965).

7 Screening by Sector

The industry-choice process is one of two, basic, intertwined processes of selection through which the pool of entrepreneurial talent available for enterprise in a given part of the economy is formed. The second process is sector choice, through which individuals select specific organizational contexts in which to work within a given industry. As for the industry-choice decision, there is more than one scenario through which the sector-choice decision may take place.

1. A potential entrepreneur may become initially employed and gain the bulk of his experience in a given sector and remain in that sector throughout his entrepreneurial phase.

2. A potential entrepreneur may gain initial experience and even undertake enterprise in one sector but eventually move on to focus the bulk of his entrepreneurial energies in another sector.

Strong inertial tendencies govern the movement of personnel who favor scenario 1 as the dominant mode. Entrepreneurs of the income-seeker, power-seeker, and searcher varieties exhibit greater inclinations toward scenario 2 than do other types. The discussion that follows treats these latter cases as if such entrepreneurs initially chose to work in the sector in which they ultimately undertake the bulk of their entrepreneurial activity.

Sectoral considerations may influence selection by industry. In particular, the predominance of a given sector within some industry is likely to affect certain structural characteristics (for example, the concentration of economic activity) on which industry selection is based. In general, however, the industry decision—which reflects a basic career choice—comes first, and sector selection is secondary, although significant. Having selected an industry, the potential entrepreneur will often have some choice of sector because most service fields are not totally dominated by a single sector.

Screening Factors

Some empirical evidence suggests systematic differences among employees in alternative economic sectors. Guyot, for example, observes that public employees are more likely to be female, come from minority group, low socioeconomic backgrounds, and to have more formal education than their private sector counterparts.[1] It is therefore reasonable to expect that the motivations of employees—latent entrepreneurs, in particular—may also differ systematically by sector.

I will proceed, as in chapter 6, by postulating a certain amount of good intuition, rational thought, and foresight on the part of potential entrepreneurs in their early choices of employment in organizations. In particular, I assert that there is a strong correlation between the motives that the entrepreneur will ultimately exhibit (when he begins to venture) and the character of organizations in which he chooses to become employed and gain experience. Thus reference to the various types of entrepreneurs—believers, power seekers, and so on—will apply to latent motivations that may not yet have become manifest but are presumably part of the individual's consciousness at the stage of choosing an organization for which to work.

The factors on which sector screening of potential entrepreneurs takes place include the following.

Opportunity. Within any given industry, some sectors tend to be larger and more vital than others at a given point in time. The relative abundance of employment opportunities will vary accordingly. For example, until the mid-twentieth century when public universities began to develop, opportunities in higher education were concentrated almost totally in the nonprofit sector. The pattern in child care is similar. For nursing homes, however, the proprietary sector has been the main locus of opportunity.

A few statistics illustrate the variety of sectoral splits among industries. According to the American Hospital Association, general hospitals were distributed across sectors in 1976 as follows: 35 percent government; 52 percent nonprofit; 13 percent proprietary. For psychiatric hospitals the figures are 59 percent, 17 percent, and 23 percent. For nursing homes the distribution was 8 percent, 19 percent, and 73 percent. In education, according to 1976 U.S. Department of Health, Education, and Welfare (HEW) statistics, elementary schools were 82 percent public and 18 percent nonpublic, whereas secondary schools were 87 percent public and 13 percent private (See Miller).[2]

In higher education, according to Nielsen, the distribution in enrollments between public and private, nonprofit institutions has gone from 50 percent each in 1950 to 78 percent versus 22 percent in favor of public institutions in 1977.[3] For medical schools in 1977, the division was 57 percent and 43 percent, in favor of public institutions.

In the day-care-center industry, according to a study by Abt Associates, approximately 41 percent of centers were profit making, compared with 59 percent nonprofit or governmental, in 1976–1977.[4] Of the 59 percent labeled nonprofit, 7 percent were governmental, 4 percent Headstart; and 3.2 percent, school affiliated.

According to Netzer, 85 percent of the arts sector (broadly defined) in terms of annual expenditure is commercial.[5] For 1971–1972, about 56 percent of museums were private nonprofit, compared with 34 percent government, 5 percent attached to public educational institutions, and 5 percent attached to private educational institutions.[6] (Proprietary galleries or exhibitions are excluded from the count.)

In the research and development industry, Dickson indicates roughly a 70 percent–30 percent division between profit-making and nonprofit or public agencies in the late 1960s and early 1970s.[7] Of the six hundred or so agencies that he considers think tanks, about half are profit making, one-third are nonprofit, and one-sixth are governmental.

In broadcasting, according to figures presented by Schutzer, public and nonprofit educational FM radio stations constituted slightly less than one-eighth of all radio stations in 1979, whereas educational television stations (VHF and UHF) represented about 25 percent of all television stations in that year.[8]

Government funding or licensing policies often underlie these patterns of sectoral distribution (see chapter 10). For example, some states refuse to certify proprietary foster-care agencies. In contrast, programs such as FHA mortgage guarantees helped underwrite the growth of proprietary nursing-home enterprise, and other legislation, for example, state higher-education programs, sponsored the specific development of public systems (universities).[9]

Although latent entrepreneurs of various types may have strong leanings by sector, they may also be limited in their ability to exercise those preferences, that is, sector choice may be constrained by existing sectoral opportunity structures within industries. If opportunities are restricted by sector, that is, if there is a mismatch between available opportunities by sector and the sector preferences of entering personnel, then some latent entrepreneurs who have selected a given field will be forced to become employed in less preferred sectors. The less preferred sectors will then include entrepreneurial types that they would not otherwise attract. Given a more open opportunity structure, latent entrepreneurs would be sorted into more homogeneous motivational sets by sector. The implications of this important phenomenon will be developed in chapter 10.

What determines if a sector is more or less preferred by a latent entrepreneur? Aside from opportunity constraints, other factors will tend to sort out the entrepreneurial types. Most of these factors, including income potential, internal bureaucratic structure, and service ethic, vary in a fairly unambiguous way from sector to sector for a wide range of industries.

Income Potential. The nonprofit sector is by definition restrained by the so-called nondistribution constraint, which formally precludes appropriation of differences between revenues and expenditures as profits by managers or trustees. As Hansmann and others argue, the existence of this constraint discourages income augmentation in the nonprofit sector by signaling what is meant by appropriate behavior and by raising the threat of legal penalties for violation of this norm. Income-increasing behavior in the nonprofit sector is not impossible or even terribly unusual, however. Devices such as the inflation of salaries and perquisites or kickback and sweetheart schemes for the purchase of other inputs are possible and observed. (See Mendelson, for example.)[10] Thus in industries whose resources are concentrated in the nonprofit sector (perhaps reflecting explicit policy or relative states of sector development, the nonprofit sector may be seriously viewed as a source of wealth enlargement.

Nonetheless, income potential is nominally more restricted and blunted in the nonprofit sector than it is in the profit sector. In the proprietary sector, income-maximizing behavior is the prescribed norm and may be legally implemented directly through profits, ownership, and appreciation of capital as well as through increases in salary and perquisites and control over input factors. Of course, the relative potentials for increasing income in the profit and nonprofit sectors will also depend on market factors, including the demand for particular services and the level of competition, and on tax and other revenue considerations. Nonprofits in some fields can conceivably combine tax concessions and access to philanthropy to generate income potentials in excess of proprietary capabilities. The appropriation of surpluses as personal income can, within wide limits, be held in check by accountability to the groups (government, donors, consumers) responsible for enforcing the conditions under which such special advantages are granted (see chapter 8).

Income potentials and expectations in the public sector are quite variable: corruption, opportunities for advancement, and remuneration levels of public employees tend to differ considerably over time and place. Significantly, in some parts of the public sector, for example, within the federal government and some state and large local governments, civil-service and political-appointee pay scales and other benefits can be sufficiently attractive to warrant the attention of those whose career objectives may center heavily on income augmentation. Alternatively, the public sector may be viewed by some as a training ground or springboard from which income-seeking careers may be launched into the private sector. Much depends on the particular political conditions associated with given parts of the public sector, including the wealth and level of demand for public goods by the relevant constituencies, the strength of public-sector unions, and the tolerance levels for corruption and conflicts of interest.

In the upper managerial ranks at least, such as assistant-commissioner or deputy-assistant-secretary levels, the public sector is often viewed as a broad vertical continuum. Hence those with long-term income-increasing goals may conceive of career ladders that begin at the local level and proceed upward through state and federal echelons, featuring increased benefits along the way. Since lateral mobility across local or state jurisdictions is fairly uncommon, however, the latent entrepreneur's view of the income potential of the public sector will be highly conditioned by his local origins. On balance, the public sector would appear to constitute a middle ground between the clear income potentials of the profit sector and the restrained income orientation of the nonprofit sector.

Bureaucratic Structure. Within a given industry, the profit-making, nonprofit, and public sectors differ in their degrees of dependence on hierarchy and political accountability and hence in the flexibility, independence, and authority that staff members and officials can maintain. For example, chapter 6 briefly noted the tendency of economic activity in service fields to become more concentrated and more hierarchical as one moves from proprietary to nonprofit to government sectors.

Concentration and hierarchy were observed to affect the selection of potential entrepreneurs by industry because of implications for power seeking, autonomy, and other motives. Within industries, a similar selection process will take place by sector.

There are several implications of hierarchy. Although large hierarchical structures may provide more opportunity for power-seeking behavior, they also tend to entail more cumbersome and restrictive internal systems of control and accountability. Those who value personal flexibility and freedom from rigid systems of rules, reporting, and authorizations, would thus prefer working in less hierarchically structured sectors. This inclination is further strengthened by the tendency of staffs of large, hierarchical organizations to develop an inertial character of their own that restricts the freedom of action of those who would promote new initiatives. As Smith explains, such problems have inspired the formation of government corporations and nonprofit agencies separate from government itself:

> [These] types of organization arose in part out of a need to have a public function performed in a more flexible administrative framework than was easily available within one of the traditional executive departments. . . . [They] initially enjoyed considerable autonomy in regard to personnel and staffing practices; the normal civil service pay scales did not apply and, consequently, employment opportunities tended to be more attractive than civil service.[11]

It is not simply the dependence on hierarchy, however, that differentiates the bureaucratic structure of the three sectors. The degree of interaction with and restraint from overseeing bodies and political entities also varies systematically by sector, with important implications for latent entrepreneurs who value autonomy and may disdain the requirement to share decision-making authority. Agencies in each sector are normally associated with a board or council of trustees in one form or another. In the public sector, a government bureau is accountable to a legislature or a sublegislative committee and often to a community-advisory board as well. Nonprofit agencies are required to have boards of directors or trustees composed of responsible community members to whom the ultimate well-being of the corporation is entrusted. These boards normally have the power to appoint the agency's executive director and to approve basic fiscal and program policy. In the proprietary sector, corporate responsibility resides in a board of directors composed of shareholders, often including the executive director. In some cases, proprietary and nonprofit agencies have additional advisory committees attached to specific program activities, often to satisfy requirements of government-funding programs in which they may be involved.

Within each sector, the authority asserted by these overseeing bodies varies considerably, perhaps most widely in the nonprofit sector. Nonprofit-agency boards of directors are known to range from those whose officers insist on major day-to-day influence on policymaking to those which are virtually rubberstamps for the executive director. The public and proprietary sectors show less variance. Legislative committees usually assume a reasonable level of control over an agency's budget and executives are normally well advised to pay homage to their legislative benefactors. In the proprietary sector, the executive usually has strong, often dictatorial control, commensurate with his financial interest and ability to keep the enterprise solvent and prosperous. Clarkson explains that nonprofit (and, by extension, public-sector) trustee control over the executive function tends to be more inhibiting than it is in the proprietary sector because output is more difficult to measure and managerial rewards are only loosely related to changes in organizational wealth.[12] Trustees of nonproprietary organizations must therefore compensate by imposing stricter rules and procedures.

Because such issues seem to amplify as one moves from commercial to private-nonprofit to governmental realms, it may be said that the requirement of executives to share authority and to be constrained by overseeing bodies increases systematically from proprietary to nonprofit to public sectors.

A similar spectrum obtains with respect to entanglement of a more general political nature. The proprietary-agency director must be careful to cultivate certain relationships to secure zoning, licensing, or other approvals that he may need for operation. He may have to be careful not to arouse community opposition to his operation if he is dealing with sensitive areas, such as services to the retarded, delinquent, or mentally ill. He may also be required to follow particular rules and reporting protocol if he decides to accept government funding. The proprietary director, however, will be fundamentally less entangled and constrained by political considerations and government regulation than his nonprofit or public-sector counterparts.

The nonprofit agency is based on the notion of a public purpose for some constituency, whether it be a particular neighborhood, ethnic or religious group, or those interested or needing a particular type of service. Its board of directors, staff, and volunteers are more likely to have roots in this constituency and to bring a strong element of political responsiveness and responsibility to the agency itself. Even those nonprofit agencies which might be incorporated without such community ties will normally be required by government to constitute a board of trustees representative of the public purpose for which nonprofit status is granted. Thus there will be at least a nominal sensitivity to political pressures and constituencies by the nonprofit. Furthermore, when the nonprofit receives public funds or is designated as a vehicle for public-service delivery, it will become enmeshed in the broader spectrum of political concerns and regulatory requirements. Meyer describes an example of both political accountability and trustee control in the case of the Metropolitan Museum of Art:

> As a result of . . . news stories, the attorney general of New York State ordered an official inquiry to determine whether the museum had deliberately ignored donor wishes. . . . Under pressure to make a full public accounting of past sales, the Metropolitan for the first time disclosed its transactions and agreed reluctantly to establish new procedures for deaccessioning. Satisfied, the attorney general absolved the museum of intent to violate the law. [Museum director] Hoving thus survived a scandal that would surely have toppled any other museum director; that he was able to do so was in good part attributable to his skill in managing the board and in retaining the support of its president, C. Douglas Dillon.[13]

By far the most overwhelming set of political constraints is faced by directors of public bureaus whose decisions must often reflect partisan, geographic, ethnic, and other political sensitivities. New policies or program initiatives must be checked or modified for their effects on multiple groups before action can be taken.

Overall, therefore, sectoral differences in organizational structure provide differential opportunities to those potential entrepreneurs whose ultimate motives concern power, autonomy, and flexibility. In general, the public sector is the most concentrated in terms of hierarchy and outside restraint on freedom of action; the proprietary sector tends to be least intense in these dimensions; and the nonprofit sector constitutes a broad middle ground.

Service Ethic. Just as the different sectors vary in the norms that they encourage with respect to money-making, they also differ in the ideals and service orientations that they espouse. Whereas such normative codes may not in themselves be powerful influences on behavior, their importance as signaling devices for latent entrepreneurs at the stage of employment choice cannot be totally ignored.

Each sector has its lofty traditions and positive self-images. As Nielsen says in his discussion of private versus public colleges, "Each of these subsectors has developed its separate (and sometimes self-glorifying) definition of itself."[14] Government has the notion of public service—devotion to country and community through the competent provision of essential services. In earlier eras, public servants—policemen, firemen, soldiers, even postmen and teachers—were heroes in the public mind, and in the managerial and political ranks, statesmanship, patriotism, and leadership were important values. In recent years, this imagery has faded, but there remains a concept of public interest that underlies the value system for government work. Although this notion is vague, it connotes selfless attention to the needs of a society or community as a whole. As such, public sector employment may still attract idealists who identify with the public-service image.

Traditionally, the profit-making sector has been the domain of the rugged individualist, the self-made man who works hard for his living and makes it on his own. It is the domain of commerce, subject to the harsh discipline of the marketplace, where activity is frankly viewed as business and only secondarily as service. It is where fortunes may be made, but where every cent must be earned, where free enterprise rules and government is viewed as an intrusive and corrupting influence. As Vladeck observes for nursing homes: "Proprietary nursing home owners are not averse to reminding legislators that they are independent, taxpaying entrepreneurs with payrolls to meet and bottom lines to be looked at."[15] In the modern era of large, multinational corporations and complex entanglements between government and private industry, this individualist image too has worn thin, yet it maintains an essence of viability, especially in the arena of small business and many service industries. This image influences latent entrepreneurs who see themselves as individualists who want to make it on their own.

The nonprofit sector has its roots in voluntarism, charity, community, and in large measure, organized religious denominations. It is a mode of organization based on the notion of voluntary mobilizaton of close-knit communities to assist those of its members in need or in trouble. Whether it is a social agency, hospital, or museum, the nonprofit agency is seen to be supported by voluntary contributions, manned by volunteers or those who work for some sacrifice in pay, controlled by community elders, and administered by those whose interests are benevolent and specifically attuned to local-community needs. As with the folklore of the other sectors, the nonprofit's idealized imagery has also been tarnished as the application of this organizational device has been modified, extended, and intertwined with other sectors over time. Still, the imagery continues to bear some semblance of fact and hence to serve as a signal to those potential employees (latent entrepreneurs) who find it appealing.

Screening of Entrepreneurs

The relatively systematic differences in income potential, bureaucratic structure, and service ethic serve to sort out latent entrepreneurs among sectors.

Income seekers will be most strongly attracted to the proprietary sector, where the avenues for money-making are more numerous and open and where profit making is a socially approved and legal mode of behavior. (See Vladeck's account on nursing homes in the 1950s and 1960s.)[16] This tendency will be modified to the degree that the market or regulatory environment restricts financial gain in the profit sector or generous income streams and salary opportunities are channeled to the nonprofit or government sectors. (See chapters 8 and 10.)

Independents will also tend to gravitate to the proprietary sector because of the less overbearing requirements in that sector for shared decision making and accountability to others, and because the lower concentration of activity in that sector provides greater opportunity for achieving positions of executive autonomy. This tendency will be modified to the extent that small nonprofits with rubber-stamp boards are able to insulate themselves from outside pressures and hence attract independents. In few cases, however, will independents be attracted to government, where hierarchical and political-accountability arrangements are omnipresent.

Power seekers will generally gravitate to the public sector for the same reasons that independents reject this alternative. Government exhibits major hierarchical structures and arenas of public visibility in which power seekers may climb to greater heights of control and notoriety. As Schaffner observes, "management in government is indeed different from management in industry. . . . High and frequent turnover in top levels of government . . . political considerations, complicated bureaucratic procedures, and media limelight all contribute to the rarefied climate in the public sector."[17] This atmosphere will be especially appealing to the bold and ambitious player-type power seeker. The controller-type power seeker is more complex, however. Whereas the opportunities for expanding control in the public sector appeal to him, at some level the public sector becomes overwhelming. Major departments become too large to control and accountability relationships too complex to manage. The latent controller type may therefore decide that organizations in the nonprofit sector present more comfortable alternatives.

The believer is most likely to be attracted by the service ethic of the nonprofit or public sectors, but his uncompromising ideas for social reform and social change are more likely to be accommodated by the less overbearing accountability structure of the nonprofit arena. Thus, the nonprofit sector is likely to employ more than its share of believers.

According to Nielsen, believerism is common across many nonprofit industrial sectors:

> In the world of the nonprofits, there is constantly present a great latent righteousness because most of the inhabitants feel they are serving some high moral purpose in behalf of the commonweal. As a result, educators, scientists, artists, and reformers can be readily aroused to assert the claims of their institutions in passionate and absolute terms. To educators, education is not only virtuous but the bedrock and precondition of democracy. . . . Scientists view the quest for knowledge . . . as essential to human advancement and well-being. . . . Those devoted to cultural activities see them as the core and very definition of civilization. . . . Likewise doctors, religious leaders, and social activists all can express the value of the work to which they have committed their lives in the most ardent and uncompromising terms.[18]

Conservers, too, are most likely to be employed in the nonprofit sector, for several reasons. First, they have a loyalty to traditions and sentimentalities more likely to be found in the nonprofit and public sectors than in the proprietary sector. (An exception here is the multi-generation family business, which may invoke conserver-type loyalties in the profit sector.) Second, conservers are more likely to be attracted by the smaller size and greater informality of organizations in the nonprofit sector, where traditions and personal relationships are more easily cultivated and maintained.

Like the power seekers, the two varieties of artist are also somewhat different in their likely employment preferences. Neither the poet or architect varieties are likely to be heavily attracted to the public sector because of their desires to use activities as personal expressions of accomplishment. In the public sector, more people are involved with specific activities because of the greater hierarchy and complexity of accountability arrangements; consequently, there is less opportunity for personal identification with the product. (Men like Robert Moses, who have managed to put their personal signature on works, are more the exception than the rule. Incumbent politicians tend to receive credit for accomplishments within their domains, whether or not they were personally responsible.) Both artist types can be accommodated by the relatively less encumbered structure of the nonprofit sector, but the poet may be more confined to this sector than the architect. The architect is more concerned with the fact *that* he is building than with *what* he is building. Hence opportunities in the profit sector, where vistas for new projects may be wide, may be as appealing as those available in the nonprofit sector. For the poet, however, activity is more a matter of personal expression of ideas and values than of structure building or pride of technique. The poet is more likely to feel inhibited by the rigor and restraint of the profit criteria and to feel more comfortable in the nonprofit sector where the diversity of support sources is more apt to be indulgent of diverse ideas, irrespective of direct-market potential (or political content).

Finally, professional- and searcher-type latent entrepreneurs will be inclined to find the nonprofit sector a comfortable middle ground, for reasons similar to those cited in the industry-selection process. For the professional, nonprofits are likely to be large enough to provide the necessary resource base and logistical support to underwrite the pursuit of disciplinary accomplishment, while less inhibiting than government in following such a chosen path. Similarly, the searcher may be attracted to the ideals of the public or nonprofit realm, but likely to become stifled by governmental hierarchy.

Figure 7–1 summarizes the nominal sorting of entrepreneurial types by sector. This sorting provides a preliminary basis for modeling nonprofit-sector behavior. If nonprofit sectors follow the general patterns of income potential, bureaucratic structure, and service ethic described above and industries in which such sectors are imbedded do not seriously constrain the opportunities for entrepreneurial employment by sector or severely screen particular types of entrepreuners into or out of the industry as a whole, then it is possible to hypothesize that nonprofit sectors are characterized by the behavioral tendencies of the entrepreneurs listed in the second column of the figure. However, this view is naive and too abstract for two reasons. First, the relative structural characteristics of nonprofit sectors do vary considerably from one industry to another, hence the pattern in figure 7–1 is not universal. Second, the postscreening behavior of entrepreneurs is influenced not only by their internal motivations but also by the constraint and accountability conditions that exist at the time of venture. Still, the behaviors implied in the screening pattern displayed in Figure 7–1 may be taken as a description of central tendency in nonprofit sectors, from which variations will be considered.

Profit		Nonprofit		Public
Income seekers	Architects	Believers	Controllers	Players
Independents		Conservers		
		Poets		
		Searchers		
		Professionals		

Figure 7–1. Nominal First Preferences of Entrepreneurs by Sector

The Permanence of Industry and Sector Screening

The early screening of potential entrepreneurs by motivation into industries and sectors of employment significantly influences the character of enterprise and behavior in a sector, because there is a notable degree of immobility of these latent entrepreneurs at later career stages when most venture activity tends to take place. Specifically, strong inertial tendencies restrict the crossing of industry and sector boundaries by potential entrepreneurs once these people have made their early career decisions. These tendencies may be stated in the form of two general propositions.

1. Entrepreneurs whose early employment history is concentrated in a particular industry will tend to undertake future ventures in that same industry. Within industries, entrepreneurs whose employment history is concentrated in a given sector will tend to undertake future activity in that same sector.

These statements apply to first-time entrepreneurs as well as to those who have already begun entrepreneurial phases of their careers. The effect will tend to be stronger for industries as a whole than for sectors within industries because adaptation to different sectoral cultures is usually easier than learning whole new technologies and economic markets.

Nevertheless, inertia exists within sectors as well. Each sector tends to have its own culture to which individuals become accustomed. The profit sector preaches efficiency; the nonprofit sector stresses voluntarism and community involvement; and government uses public service and political awareness as its frame of reference. More significantly, each sector requires different modes of operation and management (financial, personnel, and so on), which individuals master by experience and which create psychological and practical barriers to lateral movement across sectors. Thus the public-sector official becomes experienced with political considerations and bureaucratic procedure; the profit maker becomes experienced with marketing and capital financing; and the nonprofit official becomes experienced with philanthropic fund raising and dealing with community groups. As a result of these cultural and operational factors, individuals who are familiar with a given sector become oriented to maintaining their activities (and hence pursuing ventures) in that sector. This situation is least true of searchers, who have previously failed to establish a comfortable foothold in a given organizational context, and most true of conservers, whose loyalties are the most keenly developed of all entrepreneurial types. The careers of power seekers and income seekers constitute additional possible exceptions. Power seekers are likely to exhibit a climbing pattern, with each successive job representing a step upward in terms of status, position, and authority over people and resources. This ladder may involve some crossovers between sectors. For example, a power seeker may begin in a relatively small nonprofit agency, move to another, more important one, and ultimately move into government at a high level. The pattern may cross sectoral borders several times, depending on the timing of opportunities. Because significant managerial opportunities may open up earlier in one's career in the nonprofit sector, but more powerful positions may be available later at the top of the public sector, the careers of power seekers often begin in the nonprofit sector but gravitate toward government. For reasons cited earlier, this pattern more often holds for a player than for a controller.

A similar argument may be made for income seekers, but with different directional patterns. This variety of latent entrepreneur may begin his career in a public or perhaps a nonprofit agency, where initial salaries may be better and where he can gain professional experience and learn about service provision. Later, having gained experience and accumulated some capital, he may decide to move into the proprietary domain. This in not an unusual career pattern for physicians, psychologists, and even academicians with highly marketable skills (engineers and economists, for example). In the research field, Smith[19] and Dickson[20] both cite a number of instances of individuals who left nonprofit think tanks to form their own private consulting outfits.

Even for power seekers, income seekers, and searchers, however, venture itself is likely to be concentrated in a single sector, that is, sector of ultimate destination, following various sector transitions that such individuals may make earlier in their careers.

A similar inertial tendency exists at the level of particular organizations.

2. Entrepreneurs associated with a particular organization will tend to undertake future ventures within the context of that same organization. The reasoning behind this proposition is similar to that underlying the first proposition. Specifically, familiarity and identification with the value structure and operational procedures of a given agency will make it costly and disruptive for those contemplating new ventures to seek a less familiar context. Again, the stipulated tendency is strongest for the conserver and weakest for the searcher. In addition, proposition 2 holds only weakly for the independent, whose entrepreneurship will often be centered on the goal of founding a new agency under his own jurisdiction. The independent may, however, find his opportunity for entrepreneurship by assuming the helm of his current organization or by working from within to spin off an autonomous agency that he can direct.

Summary

The factors of relative opportunity, income potential, bureaucratic structure, and service ethic screen latent entrepreneurs who have selected a given

industry into alternative sectors within that industry. Sector screening tends
to be relatively permanent for individual latent entrepreneurs, although
notable exceptions have been discussed. Even these exceptions may be
analyzed as if sector choices are made by certain entrepreneurs a bit later in
their careers—after early experience has been gained but before the major
portion of entrepreneurial activity has been undertaken. Thus early industry
and sector screening still form the basic mechanisms for determining the
motivational mix for enterprise in a given sector. These motivations constitute a crucial element for determining the ultimate shape of organizational
behavioral in a sector. The constraining influences on those motivations are
considered next.

Notes

1. James F. Guyot, "Public and Private: A Distinction That Makes a
Difference" (Bernard Baruch College, City University of New York, presented to American Political Science Association, August 1980). Also, "The
Convergence of Public and Private Sector Bureaucracies" (American Political Science Association, 1979).

2. Lohr E. Miller, "A Quantitative Guide to the Nonprofit Sector of
the U.S. Economy" (Draft, Program on Nonprofit Organizations, Yale
University, March 1980).

3. Waldemar A. Nielsen, *The Endangered Sector* (New York: Columbia University Press, 1979).

4. Richard Ruopp, Jeffrey Travers, Frederic Glantz, and Craig Coelen,
Children at the Center (Cambridge: Abt Books, 1979) and, *Day Care Centers in the U.S.: A National Profile 1976–1977* (Cambridge: Abt Books,
1979).

5. Dick Netzer, *The Subsidized Muse* (Cambridge: Cambridge University Press, 1978).

6. *Museums U.S.A.: A Survey Report* (National Research Center of
the Arts for the National Endowment for the Arts, Washington, D.C. 1974).

7. Paul Dickson, *Think Tanks* (New York: Atheneum, 1971).

8. George J. Schutzer, "Prevalence of Nonprofit Organizations in the
Broadcast Media" (PONPO working paper 14, Institution for Social and
Policy Studies, Yale University, March 1980).

9. Bruce C. Vladeck, *Unloving Care* (New York: Basic Books, 1980).

10. Mary A. Mendelson, *Tender Loving Greed* (New York: Alfred A.
Knopf, 1974).

11. Bruce L.R. Smith, *The Rand Corporation* (Cambridge: Harvard
University Press, 1966).

12. Kenneth W. Clarkson, "Managerial Behavior in Nonproprietary Organizations," in *The Economics of Nonproprietary Organizations*, eds. Kenneth W. Clarkson and Donald L. Martin (Greenwich, Conn.: Jai Press, 1980).

13. Karl E. Meyer, *The Art Museum* (New York: William Morrow and Co., 1979).

14. Nielsen, *Endangered Sector*.

15. Vladeck, *Unloving Care*.

16. Ibid.

17. Robert M. Schaffner, "Can a Scientific/Technical Executive from Industry Find Happiness in a Government Agency?," in *Managing Nonprofit Organizations*, eds. Diane Borst and Patrick J. Montana (New York: AMACOM, 1977).

18. Nielsen, *Endangered Sector*.

19. Smith, *Rand Corporation*.

20. Dickson, *Think Tanks*.

8

Constraints, Constituents, and the Shape of Venture Outcomes

The set of motivations of potential entrepreneurs constitute the entrepreneurial engines potentially at work in the economy at large. The processes of screening—by sorting entrepreneurial objectives into relatively homogeneous groups—then provide a sense of the different directions in which the drivers of these engines would prefer to steer their associated ventures within different industries and sectors.

What about the roadways that these entrepreneurial trips follow? That is, how much discretion does the entrepreneur enjoy in initiating, designing, and guiding his venture to suit his own objectives, particularly within the nonprofit segments of various industries?

The roads in some sectors can be quite narrow because of the stringent nature of certain economic or social constraints. In a highly competitive profit-making sector, for example, economists argue that profit-maximizing (via the selection of certain best production and marketing strategies)is the only way to avoid being driven out of business by more efficient competitors. In the broad area of services produced by nonprofit organizations, however, the range of entrepreneurial discretion is usually much wider, and thus the diversity of entrepreneurial objectives is of concern. If constraints were so rigid that only one mode of behavior were tolerated, then such diversity would be irrelevant. According to the managerial-discretion theory of the firm pioneered by Williamson, a variety of entrepreneurial objectives can only be manifested if the economic environment is not so stringent that such indulgence threatens survival.[1] In general, however, external constraints and opportunity structures remain quite important in shaping the ultimate behavioral nature of enterprise. This chapter will consider how certain structural aspects of sectors define the bounds within which (screened) entrepreneurs may work, and how these factors shape the rationale and format, if not spirit and content, of venture possibilities.

The principal sources of restraint on entrepreneurial action are the formal (statutory) requirements on entry of new programs into a given industry and the interests and preferences of various constituent groups that exert control over policy formulation and over economic resources required to finance potential ventures. Together these sources of restraint define what may essentially be thought of as a possibility set, which constitutes the range of discretion within which an entrepreneur may design and promote his ventures.

Restraints on Entry.   Previous chapters considered the effects of governmental controls and other barriers to the establishment of new organizations
and programs on the concentration of economic activity in a given industry
or sector and hence the screening of entrepreneurs into those parts of the
economy. This chapter deals with the effects of such barriers on the activity
of entrepreneurs already screened into their respective sectors.

There are two types of cases—entrepreneurs who have been screened
into sectors consistent with their entry-related preferences, and entrepreneurs who have been screened into sectors whose entry policies conflict with
their preferences. Entry restraints may be expected to favor rather than
inhibit the kinds of venture activity preferred by the first group of entrepreneurs. Entry restraints may be expected to have two effects on the second
group: to diminish the overall level of venture activity, and to stimulate
entrepreneurial initiatives designed to circumvent the restraints.

In general, the latent entrepreneurial population within a given sector is
expected to consist largely of those whose preferences are compatible with
the entry rules. Several reasons for exceptions exist, however. First, entry
rules or requirements may change between the time an entrepreneur
chooses a given sector and industry and the time he undertakes an enterprise. Second, entrepreneurs may undergo changes in personal goals and
become immobile in terms of their sector affiliation. Third, the entrepreneurial screening process is necessarily imperfect. For instance, differential
entry conditions among sectors (see chapter 10) tend to distort the opportunity structure over the long run by reducing activity and employment levels
in one sector relative to another. Thus some latent entrepreneurs may
simply not be allowed to enter their preferred sectors. In addition, in view of
the several variables on which screening takes place, entry conditions may
not be the primary determinant of selection for many entrepreneurs, who
may therefore be screened into sectors with entry rules at odds with their
preferences. For these reasons, it is important to consider not only the
behavioral implications of entrepreneurs who have been screened into
sectors consistent with their entry-related preferences but also the behavioral implications of those who have not. In particular, certain types of
entrepreneurs who may fail to be screened into a sector with compatible
entry conditions may attempt to subvert or circumvent these requirements
in one way or another. Such entrepreneurs set in motion some of the
more interesting, albeit secondary, modes of observed venture behavior, as
follows.

Independents are likely to have screened themselves away from sectors
with imposing barriers to new entry, and those who have not been so
screened will no doubt operate at a diminished activity level. In that context,
however, independents may still attempt to create semiautonomous enclaves for themselves. They can do so in two ways. If the sector is composed

of relatively small organizations, the independent will attempt to move to the top and gain control of one of them. More likely, the restricted-entry sector will be composed of relatively large organizations; in this case the independent will try to form his own subdivision within which he can essentially be his own boss (see Young and Finch for one illustration).[2] Thus independents will work to decentralize and fragment large organizations in which they become enmeshed.

For different reasons, and at a substantially larger scale of organization, power seekers of the controller variety may act in concert with independents; that is, once organizations start to become extremely large, controllers may tolerate or even tacitly encourage spin-off behavior, divesting their organizations of semiautonomous units by setting them up as independent agencies. Such action may be feasible even in an environment of restricted entry because the controller can use the resources of the parent agency to assist in overcoming entry barriers. Alternatively, controllers who are working their way up in large organizations may behave quite similarly to independents, carving out pieces of the overall agency as semiautonomous units over which they can exert their own authority.

Power seekers in general are likely to have screened themselves into sectors with restrictions on entry where such policy has encouraged the development of large agencies. However, a power seeker who has, for other reasons, been screened into an open-entry sector will work in a manner contrary to that system. In particular, he will attempt to build up his own organization and work toward restricting entry and gaining control of other organizations. Thus power seekers, particularly players, will promote mergers, found trade associations that promulgate minimum standards, and lobby for governmental restraints on entry.

Income seekers will tend to screen themselves away from industries governed by an entry policy that confines allowable activity to the nonprofit (or public) sectors. Entrepreneurs of this type who fail to be so screened will severly test the nondistribution constraint through various mechanisms of income augmentation that substitute for owner claims on declared profits. These mechanisms may include the inflation of salaries and perquisites, kickbacks, sweetheart contracts, and other self dealing schemes associated with the purchase of inputs to production. (See Mendelson's description of certain nonprofit nursing-home entrepreneurs).[3] Clarkson, describes one sophisticated device: renting real property to nonprofits by property-owning managers, who take advantage of quick depreciation schedules, capital gains, and setting rents to extract profits while maintaining nonprofit tax status.[4]

Constituent Accountability. Various nonentrepreneurial groups associated with organizations effectively monitor and exert some control over the development of new enterprise in any given sector of the economy. These groups may be roughly divided into four, nonexclusive categories: internal, client, rival, and resource providing. The implied requirements of such constituent groups (for example, for shared decision-making participation and authority) will affect the screening process for some entrepreneurs. Such groups may also exert direct constraining effects on ventures and enterprising behavior. In particular, these constituent groups can become involved in conflicts with entrepreneurs of different persuasions and ultimately thwart certain types of venture initiative. Alternatively, the preferences of constituent groups may shape the nominal rationale but not the essential content of ventures that do go forward.

Internal interest groups consist of staff and trustees associated with organizations in which ventures are contemplated. If the venture is intended to bring radical change to an established agency—often the case in a problem-response scenario, for example—these groups may become a strong source of resistance. Staff may fear for their jobs and trustees may be sentimental over departure from traditional values or ways of doing things. The strength of these effects will vary from sector to sector, however. Proprietary agencies will tend to be the most flexible and least affected by such inertial elements because their structure concentrates power at the executive level. Furthermore, proprietary board members are primarily investors whose sentiments focus on profits more than on service objectives; hence efficiency, solvency, and managerial prerogative are traditionally maintained as the most important criteria of organizational decision-making. As long as (entrepreneurial)management has a financially successful track record, it will have a relatively free hand in implementing change or maintaining support for new enterprise.

Nonprofit agencies, on the other hand, may be substantially affected both by the sentimental loyalties of long-standing board members and by the conservative interests of staff who may have long been affiliated with the organization. As Anthony,[5] McQuade,[6] Cornuelle,[7] and others suggest, although trustees are not always especially competent, effective, or conscientious in their overseeing functions, the more pervasive shared decision-making culture of the nonprofit form often gives them substantial voice as potential restraining elements. As Meyer observes in the museum field:

> a factor that applies to nearly all the largest art museums in the United States—[is] their governance by private boards composed of the established rich who have been operating with limited accountability and who have on occasion demonstrated minimal sophistication about the arts. In enough cases to warrant generalization, the decapitation of the director has been a ritual sacrifice on the alter of his board's incompetence. . . .

> Changing times have greatly strained the traditional structure of museum management, but many—if not most—boards have been reluctant to move

with the times. . . . Directors and staff often have to struggle with an archaic system in which a single powerful trustee operates like a feudal baron.[8]

Clarkson provides a more sympathetic view, explaining that the intrinsic nature of the nonprofit and its services, for example, the lack of measurable output and a profit criterion, makes trustees' tasks more difficult.[9]

In the public sector, political and bureaucratic impediments tend to prevail, with effects similar to those that obtain as a result of the sentimentalities, administrative difficulties, and self-serving interests, that restrain the nonprofit sector. Effects in the public sector may be considerably stronger, however, because civil-service tenure systems and employee unions, bureaucratic procedures, and political sacred cows protected by legislators may severely inhibit entrepreneurial discretion.

A similar spectrum exists at the client level with respect to the rigidity of constraints across sectors. Proprietary agencies are freer, and indeed more obligated, to track the economic demand for services—as expressed by the willingness of private clients to pay or the stipulations of government fees for service programs—than are nonprofits, which receive grant funds and contributions, or government bureaus, which receive legislative appropriations. Thus proprietary agencies shift relatively quickly with the market, more easily ignoring product loyalties of current consumers.

Nonprofits usually build a more permanent relationship with the communities that they serve. These bonds are developed through various mechanisms, including citizen participation on boards and committees, donations from community members, and expressions of broad community support on which the nonprofit may have been initially established. Ventures that would disengage a nonprofit from its historical client and community roots, or otherwise change its mission significantly, can therefore face strong resistance. In a similar manner, government bureaus and program divisions also have their particular constituencies and interest groups. Those groups may have advocated the agency's programs, cultivated working relationships with its staff, and supported its appropriations in legislative hearings. Disengagement or departure from interests of current clients could, therefore, be highly problematic for the public-sector entrepreneur. As Vladeck explains, private operators can simply shut their doors or file for bankruptcy, but government, once having assumed responsibility for a given program or clientele cannot easily absolve itself of that commitment.[10] New public sector initiatives, even those involving reverses of direction, do often take place during changes of political administrations, however. If such political change reflects an underlying shift in demography, implying changes in public demands for services, it can be ignored only at the government official's peril. This situation differs from the often more stable perspective of nonprofits, whose governors have a greater tendency to adhere to historical missions even in the face of societal change.

Resource-providing constituents of a service-producing organization may include paying clients; private, third-party insurers; investors and bankers; philanthropists and small contributors; and governmental agencies that provide grants or administer fees for service programs. A proprietary agency appeals to a subset of these groups for economic support. Its clientele may include paying consumers, government agencies that finance (through fees for service) consumption by nonpaying (or part-paying) users, and third-party (insurance) agencies; its investors consist of private individuals who expect a financial return and banks that will lend funds based on the collateral of physical plant, personal finances of the entrepreneur and his backers, and the promise of future returns on investment. The demands of these various groups are unified by the overall mandate of the marketplace: subject to possible procedural and service-quality stipulations that derive from governmental regulation, the quality, cost, and distribution of services must be such as to turn a reasonable profit. Depending on the cogency and volatility of consumer versus investor support, this mandate may encourage alternative strategies of cost and quality variation. For example, if consumer demand is highly elastic with respect to quality, or if government exerts strong regulatory pressure associated with its fees for service contracts, then quality may be emphasized more than it would be otherwise. Under other circumstances, however, results differ; for example, in the nursing-home industry consumer well-being has sometimes been secondary to real-estate speculation.[11]

In the nonprofit case, resource providers may be more diverse and their mandates substantially less clear than in other sectors. Sources of operating support for nonprofits may include user, third-party, or governmental fees for services, philanthropic donations, and government grants. Returns on endowment may be a source of flexible income for a manager entrepreneur, providing some relief from constituent pressures, although even these funds may be restricted by original-donor stipulations. Because there is no individual ownership (that is, equity), capital funds must be generated though philanthropy, government grants, and borrowing. Given the nonmarket nature of much of the nonprofit's income and possible concentrations of funding control in the hands of a small group of contributors, trustees, or government agencies, entrepreneurs must at least pay lip service to the programmatic and personal goals of such agents. Philanthropists and trustees, for example, will want their own conceptions of the community interest served and may want some personal recognition as well. Government agencies will insist on adherence to legislative mandates, to specific standards and regulations, and to sensitivity to the needs of strong political constituencies. Overall, the nonprofit entrepreneur will prefer to reduce dependency on any one source, for fear of the pressures created by such dependency. For example, Netzer[12] and Meyer[13] cite the fear of donor pressures in the performing-arts and museum fields, respectively. Meyer cites the conflicts that arise when donors of art collections—as in the case of the Lehman Pavilion of the Metropolitan Museum of Art—impose demands on the recipient museums. Meyer notes that "Over the years the Metropolitan's board had evolved a policy of rejecting such binding donor requests, and it was justifiably feared that in acceding to the Lehman terms, the museum would encourage other wealthy collectors to be as demanding."

Netzer reviews the experience of the Arena Stage Theater:

> Arena is wary about local private support. Zelda Fichandler considers community residents the most conservative of benefactors and those likely to be hostile to controversial and experimental theater: "I am not very strong on community giving, except perhaps when it represents only a small percentage of the total. I think we could well do without the hand that rocks the cradle, for the hand that rocks the cradle will also want to raise it in a vote and mix into the pie with it. . . . So, then let the money be given at a distance, once removed, and let it be awarded by a jury of one's peers, let the audience be the only judge."

One important source of relief, and hence discretion, for nonprofit entrepreneurs is that few constituents will have direct knowledge of performance, much time for monitoring, or precise criteria for judgment. For example, Kanter observes:

> products or specific benefits do not tend to be available to donors . . . and therefore performance criteria for resource allocation (service delivery) might be unrelated to criteria for resource attraction.[14]

The same may be said of government funders or third-party agents. Furthermore, as Brinkerhoff[15] and Kanter[16] suggest, the multiplicity of resource providing and other constituencies of the nonprofit may lead to conflicts and internal bargaining. Such conflicts, combined with informational difficulties, may leave substantial opportunity for isolating these constituents from managerial and entrepreneurial decisionmaking. Kanter argues:

> In nonprofit organizations where there is a wide gap between the incentives, personnel, and procedures for resource attraction and the personnel and procedures for resource allocation, or service delivery, we can expect either a high degree of conflict in the organization (reflected in arguments about performance measures) or attempts to insulate donors or funders from allocators or deliverers, (reflected in statements about professionalism and the need for independence), which tends to reduce the willingness to have performance measured at all.[17]

Brinkerhoff, citing Shapiro's study of Boys Town, goes even further to suggest the possible consequences of such tendencies:

> This separation of resource acquisition and program operation also can result in situations where a nonprofit organization is effective in the resource attracting arena but not in the programmatic one, or vice versa.[18]

Alternatively, some view the loose accountability structure of nonprofits as more a strength than a weakness. According to Douglas:

> The absence of strong measures of accountability, far from being a weakness of the Third Sector, becomes a strength enabling it to undertake experiments, the benefits of which are too uncertain and too long term to be undertaken by either the commercial or the governmental sector.[19]

These complexities of nonprofits often provide substantial room for entrepreneurial maneuvering and discretionary management of ventures once they are under way, but these same elements of information ambiguity, conflict, and separation of revenues from allocation may inhibit entrepreneurs' abilities to gather constituent support to launch their ventures.

Mandates for ventures of public-sector agencies tend to be most rigidly defined among those of the three sectors. Whereas the entrepreneur may have been instrumental in lobbying for and shaping the authorizing legislation and appropriations, little formal discretion may remain once the specific laws are in place. Even more than nonprofits, public-sector agencies experience a separation of resource acquisition from service delivery, and limited performance information flows to resource-providing constituents, including legislative committees and taxpayers. Furthermore, legislative committees tend to be preoccupied with diverse matters and topics of current political concern and hence are relatively lax in monitoring the specific administration of authorized programs. The result may be a substantial degree of inefficient operation or even fraud, but little in the way of new directions that require substantial shifts in the use of resources or the definition of policy. Exceptions to this rule occur where governmental managers are able to act like directors of nonprofit agencies, developing close relationships with legislators as if they were board members and seeking grant funds from outside as well as within the home-government structure. This situation is most likely to occur in small governments at the local level.

Rival groups that may effectively oppose or limit new enterprise also vary by sector. In the proprietary sector, rivals principally take the form of economic competitors, that is, other agencies whose effects are felt through the impersonal workings of the marketplace and the price system. In regulated sectors new entry or expansion may be opposed by community groups through political lobbying with regulatory agencies on the basis of need-and-necessity arguments or in terms of other aspects of public interest. For example, (proprietary) homes for the mentally ill often incur opposition on the basis of disruption to the integrity or well-being of neighborhoods.

In the nonprofit sector, the latter kinds of regulatory mechanisms are even more likely to be used, for two reasons. First, nonprofits depend more directly on their local communities for sustenance and support. Indeed, the legitimacy of a nonprofit agency itself depends on its maintaining a stance consistent with community interests. To the degree that trustees, contributors, and government-funding agencies reflect local political concerns, these will be expressed within the framework of intraagency decision making. To the extent that such concerns are not represented directly by agency constituents, they may be reflected through the wider mechanisms of regulatory control and political accountability, on the basis of the nonprofit's implicit responsibilities to the public at large—especially if the nonprofit is a recipient of public funds, tax concessions, or community-wide charities, such as the United Fund.

The second source of rivalry in nonprofit venture may come from implicit competitive pressures within the sector. Although nonprofit sectors tend to shun explicit competition in favor of interagency coordination[20] and to organize themselves into basically cooperative milieus that feature relatively open exchange of information, cross-referrals of clients, networking arrangements of various kinds,[21] community planning, and even joint ventures, some forms of new enterprise may be perceived as a threat to members of such a sector. For example, a venture of one agency that threatens to reduce the share of activity by other agencies will be viewed askance.

Similarly, a new agency's entry on the limited turf of existing agencies is likely to be skeptically received by those agencies. Nonprofits disdain competition and rivalry as a rule, and as a group are willing to engage in cooperative efforts that promise to maintain the status of individual agencies and to serve some public purpose. They will tend also to join forces in opposition, using regulatory and political channels, when a new venture is posed by some individual agency in a threatening way. Such action can be extremely effective because the board members and other representatives of rival nonprofits are often influential members of the community and well connected both politically and economically.

A final source of competitive resistance to nonprofit ventures may emanate from other sectors, especially if such ventures threaten to exploit the special advantages of nonprofit status and are thus viewed as unfair competitors. As reviewed by Smith, for example, this situation has occurred in the research field, particularly where government has actively funded and helped set up nonprofit research agencies.

> Another source of discontent centers in various industrial circles. A comment by Ralph H. Cordiner is typical: "However generous their motives, these nonprofit organizations are usurping a field traditionally served by private consulting firms and producer companies, and hence are little more than a blind for nationalized industry competing directly with private enterprise—on a subsidized, non-taxpaying basis."[22]

Constituent groups affect entrepreneurial initiatives not only by imposing limits and restraints but also by helping to define the rationale under which new ventures are posed. That is, board members, clients, and resource providers may all have their own ideas and preferences with respect to the purposes of organizations and programs. For certain types of entrepreneurs, constituent preferences for having ventures serve a particular purpose or rationale pose few problems. (See figure 8–1.) Independents, architects, power seekers, and income seekers in particular are relatively value free, or indifferent, with respect to the intrinsic nature of services or the intended clientele of proposed ventures. These entrepreneurial types will therefore design and advertise their ventures to the nominal tune of constituents, so long as their underlying objectives for income, power, autonomy, or building and creating can be met. Difficulties will occur, however, where expansive tendencies begin to impinge on the interests of rival agencies (as noted above) or where the service requirements of constituent groups are, in practice, simply used by the entrepreneur as a facade for the pursuit of self-serving ends and are so grossly neglected as to become obvious even to the poorly informed. Thus, within limited constituent abilities to monitor and hold ventures accountable:

> Independents may set up enterprises to maximize their own autonomy and insularity and resist desirable expansion or provision of new ser-

Value free		Concept bound
Income seekers	Searchers	Believers
Power seekers	Conservers	Professionals
Independents		Poets
Architects		

Figure 8–1. Rigidity of Entrepreneur Positions with Respect to Content of Ventures

vices that would entangle them in more complex organizational relationships.

Architects may propose and build programs beyond the legitimate needs of client groups.

Income seekers may sacrifice program quality, engage in fraudulent practices, or avoid loss-making activities that would reduce their net revenues (and hence personal-income potentials).

Power seekers may use discretionary resources to promote their own visibility or enlarge their bureaucratic empires rather than optimize service arrangements.

In nonprofit sectors especially, there tends to be a large margin for discretionary behavior of these varieties, despite the potential constituent antipathy that such behavior might arouse. The relatively indirect and part-time control exerted by constituent groups, the imprecise criteria that such groups can apply, and the separation of resource acquisition from resource allocation are the main reasons for this discretion.

In contrast to the motives of the value-free entrepreneurial types, other types are strongly tied to specific rationales for enterprise. Hence they may openly conflict with constituent groups with respect to venture purpose and style of operation rather than adapt to, or even subvert, constituent preferences. The believer is the best example. The believer will operate by attempting to draw like-minded constituents to his side, rather than obfuscate or seriously compromise his purpose through adaptation to the preferences already in place. For this reason, the believer leans toward forming new agencies rather than adapting to the machinery of existing ones.

The professional, particularly one in a scientifically oriented field, presents a similar example. To advance in his discipline, this variety of entrepreneur may lean heavily toward proving, testing, or demonstrating ideas and new concepts through model venture initiatives. Constituents may be less interested in ideas or research than in servicing clientele or community groups. Tensions can easily develop, pitting the preference of professionals for small, controlled, but well-publicized and documented, demonstrationlike programs with sophisticated research and measurement components against the preferences of constituents for programs that use resources in a manner that is less sophisticated but more responsive to immediate community needs. The fate of ventures may thus rely heavily on the professional's ability to convince constituents of the ultimate social or economic merit of his methods.

The poet may be as strong-minded as the professional and perhaps as impassioned as the believer. Although he pursues the implementation of ideas as more of a personal creative act than a formal disciplinary matter or religiously held belief, the poet may nonetheless encounter the same sources of conflict with constituent groups and be similarly unwilling to compromise.

The rationale for ventures initiated by believers, poets, and professionals will strongly reflect the intrinsic preferences of these entrepreneurial types. Constituent groups can be expected to achieve less ostensible influence on venture design for these types than for the value-free types, but whatever compromise is achieved by constituents will tend to be substantive and clearly labeled. The value-free types are more likely to accept whatever nominal rationale constituencies prefer, but to shape organizational behavior to their own ends, in less apparent ways.

Searchers and conservers constitute somewhat different cases of interaction between the pursuit of own motives and adherence to desires of constituents. The searcher is an outsider who is looking for the right sets of constituents—those who will accept him and give him a sense of purpose, yet who will promote values with which he can live. Like the believer, he will reject sources of constituent support that make him uncomfortable, but unlike the believer, he needs to find a constituent group that will help him define a mode of service that he can pursue. Thus the searcher may either attach himself to an existing organization or once having discovered a latent coalition and set of resources capable of supporting a venture in some new area of service, he may organize a new set of constituents.

Of all the entrepreneurial types, the conserver is least likely to conflict with his organizational environment. His objectives will be those of the organization that he seeks to preserve, and his perspective will thus be consistent with key constituent groups. However, the conserver may be faced with the need to reconcile conflicts among constituents—for example, between the staff and board members who wish to change the organization least and the new consumer groups or resource providers that have shown concern for the agency's performance and may have begun to withdraw support or make new demands.

In summary, the constraining forces on enterprise that derive from entry controls and the preferences and monitoring of various constituent groups affect sectoral behavior in two principal ways.

1. They help shape and define the rationale and nominal purposes for which a venture may be undertaken within a given sector.
2. They limit the discretion with which entrepreneurs can utilize ventures to pursue their own personal ends.

Effect 1 may subdue or limit the activity levels of certain concept-oriented entrepreneurial types (believers, poets, professionals) whose values may explicitly conflict with certain constituencies or performance criteria. Effect 2 may restrain the excesses of entrepreneurs, particularly value-free types (income seekers, power seekers, independents, architects), whose motivations are less explicitly identified with particular venture rationales or client interests.

The two constraint effects appear to vary substantially across sectors. In the proprietary sector, constituent pressures clearly lean in the direction of financial performance, and profitability serves as a fairly unambiguous and precise criterion that constituents (investors) can use to hold entrepreneurial discretion in check. Thus the rationale for venture must reflect paying constituents (individual clients, government, or other funding sources), and operations must generate a reasonable return to capital. Within such a context only, entrepreneurs may engage in discretionary (autonomy-seeking, self-aggrandizing, or other) behavior.

In the government sector, constituent pressures appear to constrain the nominal rationale and operational guidelines for entrepreneurial activity less effectively than in the commercial sector, but still fairly severely. Most important, new initiatives must meet tests of political acceptability before they can go forward. However, performance criteria are imprecise, performance information is poor, and accountability to resource-providing constituents is indirect and fragmented, permitting a considerable degree of entrepreneurial self-indulgence once programs are well under way.

In the nonprofit sector, there is substantially more diversity of restraints than in the public or profit-making sectors. Neither market nor political criteria are overriding, although both may be reflected within the framework of nonprofits that depend on both paying customers and governmental allocations. In addition to these sources of funds, however, the nonprofit entrepreneur has the option to pursue grants from donors and foundations as well as contributions from the public at large. Even within some industries practices range from total reliance on government funding to cases in which such reliance is negligible. Thus funds may be sought from sources whose motivations align more easily with entrepreneurial objectives (people with similar ideas or leanings, willing to back them up with financial support). A nonprofit entrepreneur with program-specific values, that is, the believer, poet, or professional, may therefore have more opportunity to shape his own enterprise than he might in other sectors, where his design must appeal to current political realities or consumer tastes. In a similar vein, the value-free entrepreneurial types also have more of an open field in which to experiment with venture rationales that can attract alternative sources of support (market, government, and voluntary).

Once under way, ventures in the nonprofit sector suffer a dearth of specific performance criteria similar to that of government programs. The market test will apply to a degree, because nonprofits must show a balanced budget and may depend in part on sales or memberships, but this criterion avoids the issue for venture supporters, such as agents of philanthropy or government, who are asked to fill in the gaps between sales revenues and expenditures. Moreover, the rationale for nonprofit ventures may be specifically counter to market success, for example, service to groups unable to pay for needed services. Nor do political criteria (who gets what) or legislative mandates fully apply, as the nonprofit can cite its diversity of support and semimarket obligations as the basis of its right to independence and self-determination. In essence, then, subject to minimal performance levels imposed (insisted upon) by various constituents groups and the necessity for a balanced budget, nonprofit ventures often operate under vague performance criteria and loose control by any given group or coalition. As such, they leave substantial room for discretionary behavior by entrepreneurs, who may indulge in self-defined motives and goals.

Notes

1. Oliver Williamson, *The Economics of Discretionary Behavior* (Chicago: Markham, 1967).

2. Dennis. R. Young and Stephen J. Finch, *Foster Care and Nonprofit Agencies* (Lexington, Mass.: Lexington Books, D. C. Heath and Company, 1977).

3. Mary A. Mendelson, *Tender Loving Greed* (New York: Alfred A. Knopf, 1974).

4. Kenneth W. Clarkson, "Managerial Behavior in Nonproprietary Organization," in *The Economics of Nonproprietary Organization,* eds. Kenneth W. Clarkson and Donald L. Martin (Greenwich, Conn.: Jai Press, 1980).

5. Robert N. Anthony, "Can Nonprofit Organizations be Well Managed?" In *Managing Nonprofit Organizations*, eds. Diane Borst and Patrick J. Montana (New York: AMACOM, 1977).

6. Walter McQuade, "Management Problems Enter the Picture at Art Museums," *Managing Nonprofit Organizations*, eds. Diane Borst and Patrick J. Montana (AMACOM, 1977).

7. Richard C. Cornuelle, *Reclaiming the American Dream* (Westminster, Md.: Random House, 1965).

8. Karl E. Meyer, *The Art Museum* (New York: William Morrow and Co., 1979).

9. Clarkson, "Managerial Behavior."

10. Bruce C. Vladeck, *Unloving Care* (New York: Basic Books, 1980).

11. Ibid.

12. Dick Netzer, *The Subsidized Muse* (Cambridge: Cambridge University Press, 1979).

13. Meyer, *Art Museum.*

14. Rosabeth Moss Kanter, "The Measurement of Organizational Effectiveness, Productivity, Performance,and Success" (PONPO working paper 8, Institution for Social and Policy Studies, Yale University, 1979).

15. Derick W. Brinkerhoff, "Review of Approaches to Productivity, Performance, and Organization Effectiveness in the Public Sector: Applicability to Non-Profit Organizations" (PONPO working paper 10, Institution for Social and Policy Studies, Yale University, 1979).

16. Kanter, "Organizational Effectiveness."

17. Ibid.

18. Brinkerhoff, "Approaches to Productivity."

19. James Douglas, "Towards a Rationale for Private Non-Profit Organizations" (PONPO working paper 7, Institution for Social and Policy Studies, Yale University, April 1980).

20. Susan Rose-Ackerman, "The Charity Market: Paying Customers and Quality Control" (PONPO working paper 19, Institution for Social and Policy Studies, Yale University, July 1980).

21. Seymour B. Sarason, Charles F. Carroll, Kenneth Maton, Saul Cohen and Elizabeth Lorentz, *Human Services and Resource Networks* (San Francisco: Jossey-Bass, 1977). See also Edward W. Lehman, *Coordinating Health Care* (Beverly Hills: Sage Publications, 1975).

22. Bruce L.R. Smith, *The Rand Corporation* (Cambridge: Harvard University Press, 1966).

9 Success and Long-Run Character of Ventures

Entrepreneurial influence is no doubt strongest at the birth of a venture and may decline thereafter. For example, in his case study of the founding of a medical school, Kimberly notes that although knowledge of the entrepreneur and his values and objectives is essential for an understanding of an organization, the importance of the person at the top diminishes in explaining organization outcomes as that organization matures.[1]

Drucker's review of the histories of Harvard and Columbia universities is also relevant:

> [Charles W.] Eliot, at Harvard (1869–1909) saw the purpose of the university as that of educating a leadership group with a distinct "style." His Harvard was to be a "national" institution rather than the parochial preserve of the "proper Bostonian" that Harvard College had been. . . . [Nicholas] Butler, at Columbia (1902–1945) . . . saw the function of the university as the systematic application of rational thought and analysis to the basic problems of a modern society. . . . These founders' definitions did not outlive them. Even during the lifetime of Eliot and Butler, for instance, their institutions escaped their control and began to diffuse objectives and to confuse priorities. . . . Yet the imprint of the founders has still not been totally erased. It is hardly an accident that the New Deal picked faculty members primarily from Columbia and Chicago to be high level advisors and policymakers . . . [while] the Kennedy Administration [which] came in with an underlying belief in the "style" of an "elite," . . . naturally turned to Harvard.[2]

Organizations do continue to reflect their entrepreneurs, while those entrepreneurs are in charge and to a degree thereafter as well. Thus it is justified to view entrepreneurs not merely as ephemeral or transient agents in an organization's life but as fundamentally influential actors who set the tone of activity for substantial periods of time. It is also useful to examine the nature of long-term entrepreneurial influence in more detail—to ask if different brands of entrepreneurship (types of entrepreneurs) affect long-run organization and sector activity in different ways and in different degrees of intensity. If so, the entrepreneurial screening processes can be expected to differently influence the long-run stability and dependability of organizations in alternative sectors.

The long-run success of an enterprise and the degree to which it continues to reflect its original intent appears to be directly related to the length of time that the entrepreneur remains committed to it. Consider the extreme

121

example of American dance companies. "The Jose Limon Dance Company was formed in 1946. . . . Limon's death (in 1972) left the company in a unique position in the history of American dance. Never before had a major American dance company, ballet or modern, continued beyond the death of its founder and principal choreographer. The Limon company is the first to do so."[3] Cornuelle observes for nonprofits in general that "The know-how often stays at its points of origin. Look at Saul Alinsky's conquest of America's worst slum, at Henry Viscardi's success in putting the handicapped to work, at Cleo Blackbrin's work in rebuilding slums, at the Meningers' work in mental health, at Millard Robert's work in education. These operations rarely reach far beyond what these gifted and strong-willed men can do themselves."[4]

In cases observed by the author, entrepreneurial influence diminished and ventures all seem to have suffered from the inability of the primary entrepreneurs to nurture them on a full-time or long-run basis. In most other cases, however, where entrepreneurs were able to concentrate their attentions on their ventures over a substantial period, the enterprises struggled much less and remained truer to original purposes. In a few cases, success was attributable to the stable guidance of the entrepreneur coupled with the commitment of hand-picked administrators to assume control and to carry on the original intent beyond the continued involvement of the entrepreneur.

The connection between entrepreneurial commitment and long-run outcome prompts the question: Are different varieties of entrepreneur more or less likely to give long-term attention to their ventures or to establish conditions under which they will be competently administered and remain true to original purpose? The answer is yes—the entrepreneurial types may be characterized according to their degrees of long-run commitment for a given venture. This venture-specific notion must be distinguished from general commitment to enterprising, however. Some kinds of entrepreneurs, although loosely dedicated to a given venture over the long term, are heavily committed to enterprising itself. Thus there are really two extremes:

1. Entrepreneurs who tend to be committed over the long run to particular ventures (long-term venturers).
2. Entrepreneurs who tend to be loosely committed to particular ventures but dedicated to enterprising as an ongoing activity (short-term venturers).

Each entrepreneurial character may be classified along the spectrum from 1 to 2, clustering at the extremes (see figure 9–1).

Long-term venturers include independents, believers, conservers, ar-

Short-Term venturers				Long-term venturers
Income seekers	Poets	Searchers	Controllers	Believers
Players	Professionals			Conservers
				Independents
				Architects

Figure 9–1. Classification of Entrepreneurs by Degree of Long-Term Commitment to Ventures

chitects, and, possibly, controllers. Independents are essentially one-time venturers who, having established their autonomous enclaves, will simply act to maintain them into the indefinite future. Conservers are of a similar nature; having come to the rescue of a cherished institution, the conserver will also continue to exert his efforts and retain responsibility for maintaining it on an even keel. Controllers resemble independents but are somewhat less reliable in terms of long-term commitment. The controller will be tempted to move from one venture to a larger one until he arrives at one that tests his limits, sense of security, and viability of central control. At that point he resembles the independent, seeking largely to maintain that enterprise in balance.

The believers and architects tend to create venture frameworks within which they can *continue* to innovate and build according to a consistent structure or idea. The believer, for example, will establish an agency or program centered on a singular idea or mission, but may continue to expand or elaborate on this theme with further ventures. The success of the mission is of paramount importance to the believer, and all his efforts go into maintaining its viability and elaborating on it.

The architect is especially committed to continual elaboration of his enterprise, but this requires maintenance of the structural foundations as well. Although the architect will be substantially more flexible than the believer in adjusting the rationale for ventures to suit changes in the environment, he will remain committed to a given venture as long as it maintains the potential for growth and experimentation. The pride with which the architect can trace his impact to the venture's roots is a fundamental source of his satisfaction.

The long-term commitment to a venture's initial rationale or mission, compared with its economic well-being, provides a contrast not only between the believer and the architect, but also among other types as well. In particular, the independent and the controller will strive to maintain economic viability, showing flexibility of mission where necessary. To the contrary, conservers may resemble believers somewhat in their commitment to original purpose; conservers are strongly concerned about the maintenance of both mission and economic stability.

Short-term venturers include income seekers, players, and, to a lesser degree, poets and professionals. Income seekers and players are essentially opportunists, willing to abandon one venture for another if better opportunities arise to increase their personal wealth or power. Hence their commitments to a given venture, its integrity of purpose or its long-term economic well-being, will be precarious. So long as alternative opportunities do not call, income-seeking and power-seeking players will stress the economic growth of their enterprises, following whatever path the environment makes most lucrative (in the case of income seekers) or most socially noteworthy (in the case of players). If attractive alternative opportunities for venture arise, however, these entrepreneurial types will be quickest to move on. The income seekers will leave first. The player, as a public-oriented personality, depends heavily on keeping his reputation unblemished. He will therefore take some pains to avoid abrupt abandonment of an enterprise whose failure may be blamed on him. The player will work to establish a credible transitional arrangement that would absolve him of any culpability should the venture founder after he leaves.

The poet and the professional are short-term venturers in the sense that their attention spans for a given enterprise depend on the venture's level of intellectual or emotional novelty or freshness. The professional is intent on working at the frontier of current disciplinary thought and knowledge generation. His ventures tend to have an experimental or demonstration quality to them, especially in industries governed by scientific disciplines. Such ventures are kept relatively small and controlled, studied intently, described at professional conferences, and written up in the literature. Given the changing currents of disciplinary thinking, however, a particular venture is unlikely to command professional attention for very long. New schools of thought or innovative ideas gradually but continually emerge, requiring the professional to move on to new forms of experimentation within a relatively short time.

The poet also has a relatively short attention span and a chronic need to explore new avenues of experience. Rather than key himself to the currents of disciplinary activity (like the professional), however, the poet is more of a free spirit, driven internally to move away from ventures that have reached a plateau of initial success and preferring to undertake some new experience. Of all entrepreneurial types, the poet is most likely to disdain the managerial role, preferring to coax, catalyze, and cajole others to contribute to and manage the new enterprise. If ventures require the poet to manage for a while, that responsibility will be assumed only reluctantly until a managerial team can be put into place. Professionals will also behave this way, to a more limited extent, preferring to establish, oversee, contemplate, evaluate, and publicize ventures rather than directly administer them. As a result, programs and agencies established by poets or professionals will tend to lose their initial flavor after a while. Such ventures will either founder after their entrepreneurs move on or they will shed their innovative, experimental tone as more conventional management assumes long-term responsibility.

Finally, the searcher is the least predictable of entrepreneurial types in terms of his long-term commitment to venture. Two conflicting effects exist in his case. On the one hand, a searcher may undergo long periods of exploration and restlessness during which he may dabble in a number of ventures. Like the poet, a searcher in this phase cannot be depended on for long-term leadership and ventures that he establishes face an uncertain future. On the other hand, a searcher will grasp tenaciously to his venture, once having found his true calling. At this point, the searcher begins to resemble the believer or independent and may be counted on to provide long-term commitment.

In summary:

1.   Sectors that attract (through screening) entrepreneurs of the believer, independent, controller, conserver, or architect varieties are likely to exhibit long-term behavior consistent with original entrepreneurial motivations. This behavior will consist of:

Agencies exhibiting long-term, relatively rigid mission orientations (believers).

Small to moderately sized (or decentralized) groups of stable, insulated agencies (independents and controllers).

Conservative, old-line, stable agencies (conservers).

Growing, expansive, dynamic agencies with multiple programs adaptive to the current economic environment (architects).

2.   Sectors that attract income seekers, players, poets, and professionals will exhibit more dynamic short-run behavior but less consistency and stability over the long run than sectors that attract other types.

Sectors that attract income seekers and players will be faster to respond to economic opportunities, but also faster to modify and abandon ventures as the external structure of opportunities changes. Hence agencies in sectors with these types of entrepreneurs are likely to undergo substantial fluctuations of both nominal purpose and economic well-being.

Sectors that attract professionals and poets will be fast to shape and develop new ideas and translate them into working programs. However, such sectors are not likely to exhibit very long-term commitments to such programs, but rather will move slowly from one set of ideas to another over time.

Real sectors will, of course, tend to attract varying mixes of entrepreneurial motivations according to the industry- and sector-structure variables discussed in chapters 6 and 7. Thus correlation of long-run entrepreneurial continuity with nonprofit-organization and sector behavior is a complex task.

Those entrepreneurial types with the strongest tendencies toward long-term consistent venture commitment—the believers and conservers—will gravitate to the nonprofit sector, whereas those with the strongest transient tendencies—the income seekers and power seekers—will tend to concentrate outside the nonprofit sector. This overall pattern is by no means rigid, however. Aside from the variations across industries in these nominal screening patterns, the relatively short-run-oriented poets and professionals also tend to inhabit the nonprofit sector more than other sectors. Still, the analysis here of long-run entrepreneurial commitments is roughly consistent and even enlightening of the observation that nonprofit sectors lean toward the more stable and trustworthy varieties of category 1 behavior, while foregoing some degree of the dynamism and unreliability of category 2. This observation is considered more fully in the next chapter, where venture-commitment considerations are integrated with other aspects of entrepreneurial behavior to derive a more general outlook on nonprofit-sector performance.

Notes

1. John R. Kimberly, "Issues in the Creation of Organizations: Initiation, Innovation and Institutionalization," *Academy of Management Journal*, December 1979.

2. Peter F. Drucker, "Managing the Public Service Institution," *The Public Interest* (Fall 1973).

3. "Centerpiece," Program Notes, Jose Limon Dance Company Program (Fine Arts Center, State University of New York at Stony Brook, September 27, 1980).

4. Richard C. Cornuelle, *Reclaiming the American Dream* (Westminster Md.: Random House, 1964).

10 Behavior and Policy

The theoretical framework of motives and constraints, screening processes, and circumstances for venture developed in previous chapters can now be applied in a normative way. This chapter will evaluate, according to a set of general social-performance criteria, the behavior of nonprofit organizations and the service industries in which they participate under alternative circumstances in the economic and regulatory environment. More specifically, it will consider the social-performance implications of alternative public policies that would change that environment.

The discussion follows three steps. First is a review of some of the key social-performance concerns or criteria that commonly pervade policy discussions pertaining to the nonprofit sector. The second step is to summarize the behavioral patterns implicit in the activity of the various entrepreneurial stereotypes in a manner that relates these behavior modes to the performance dimensions. The final step is to develop the performance implications of particular public policies by analyzing how such policies affect the screening and post screening activity of nonprofit entrepreneurial characters, and hence the mix of behavior patterns that result for sectors and industries.

Performance Issues

Within present limits of social-science knowledge, application of a single global criterion of social welfare is untenable; it is simply too overwhelming or oversimplified to ask whether one or another set of conditions that describe the nonprofit sector makes society better or worse off. The approach taken here is to reference some of the more salient concerns articulated by those who use and pay for the services of nonprofit organizations or have studied their history of service delivery. Within this context, four performance issues—some not precisely delineated in the literature but nonetheless frequently raised in discussion—stand out as relevant to this analysis.

Trustworthiness. The notion that nonprofits are in some sense more trustworthy than their proprietary and perhaps public-sector counterparts underlies the rationale developed by various scholars for the existence and utilization of nonprofit agencies. Trustworthiness basically denotes the reli-

127

ability with which an agency can be expected to pursue and protect the interest of consumers and contributors in the absence of direct client or constituent supervision. Trustworthiness involves both the fulfillment of promises, that is, delivery of services as advertised, and abstinence from fraud and depreciation of quality as strategies for self-aggrandizement. As Vladeck observes, the relationship between dishonesty and quality can be subtle:

> officials in the office of the New York Special Prosecutor insist that they have found no systematic relationship between the extent of stealing and poor care. In fact, they found that many of the biggest crooks ran moderate to very good nursing homes, while some of those who ran poor nursing homes were more incompetent than dishonest. Officials in other states have reported similar observations. The most intelligent and farsighted crooks might endeavour to run especially good facilities in order to maintain good relations with regulatory authorities, stay out of the public eye, and develop a positive professional reputation.[1]

Nonetheless, in this book's terminology, a strategy of dishonesty coupled with a facade of good quality would constitute nontrustworthy behavior. Much of the argument in favor of nonprofits as agents of trust centers on the administrative barriers to misconduct imposed by the nondistribution constraint. John Simon, referring to Hansmann's work, explains:

> the rule that prevents the managers of nonprofits from retaining profits, limits their incentives to exploit the underinformed consumer or underinformed donor; the rule, in other words, provides some basis for permitting that consumer or donor to place trust in the organization and its promises. That trust acts as a kind of substitute for the protection the well-informed consumer can obtain for himself in an orthodox market situation.[2]

It is also argued, however, that the nature of motivations screened into the nonprofit sector influences an agency's trustworthiness as much as the vigor with which the nondistribution and other constraints are enforced. Vladeck writes:

> Whatever the enforcement mechanisms, laws work best when people would behave as the law commands them to even were there no law.[3]

Thus proponents of nonprofit provision assert that participants in nonprofit agencies tend to have personal goals and attitudes more consistent with maintaining the quality and integrity of services than do participants in other sectors and for this reason are more trustworthy.

Responsiveness. An argument often heard against utilization of nonprofit (and sometimes public) organizations as vehicles for delivery of services is that they are slow to respond to demands for new or expanded services or to change their portfolio of services in response to pressures of the marketplace or government funding agencies. Nonprofits are sometimes accused of going their own way, unmindful of global societal needs. Consider Cornuelle's indictment:

> The independent sector seems to drift, moving blindly and without discipline. Its power lies raw and undeveloped. If often seems listless, sluggish, passive, and defensive. The commercial and government sectors have outrun it.[4]

Profit-making agencies, on the other hand, are said to be driven more easily toward rapid response through the lure of income. Vladeck's and Dunlop's[5] documentations of the nursing-home industry provide a more dramatic and extensive illustration. Vladeck sees the nursing-home experience in the following way:

> precisely because they are profit-seeking, for-profit firms tend to be more responsive to economic inducements provided by governments in the hope of expanding the provision of services. Public policy largely succeeded in one of its major, even if misconceived, objectives—rapid and dramatic expansion in the availability of nursing home beds—by providing more-than-adequate . . . inducements for the investment of private capital. Nonprofit organizations, whose objectives are more complex and more cross-pressured and which are probably less able to respond rapidly to anything, rise to the bait much more slowly. Indeed, nonprofit hospitals by and large failed to respond at all to repeated government efforts. . . . to get them into the long term care business.[6]

The causes of observed sluggishness of nonprofit agencies are open to some debate. Vladeck cites both external capital constraints and internal motivational factors in the nursing-home industry.[7] Dunlop stresses nonprofit decision-making procedures:

> Because of their typically more cumbersome administrative and fund-raising mechanisms . . . nonprofit providers, on average, take considerably longer to move on the application and construction process than do proprietary interests. As a consequence . . . the latter . . . moved in quickly with their formal plans to meet almost all of the anticipated bed shortage . . . before the nonprofits were ready to submit an application.[8]

Whatever the causes, when shortages of certain services exist or when new public priorities are adopted, government often seeks to rapidly increase available capacity, whether in nursing homes, day-care centers, services to the handicapped, or other essential areas. In such circumstances, the responsiveness issue tends to become a prominent, if not paramount, public concern.

Efficiency. In times of economic prosperity, when society can indulge in the search for solutions to pressing social needs (health, education) or in the fulfillment of social goals (arts, research), the responsiveness criterion tends to dominate public debate. In more stringent times, however, the generation of new service capacities is not the principal concern. The control of expenditures within existing service modes or substituting new, cheaper service modes for old ones, for example, replacing residential care with homemaker services, is of greater concern. One need only compare the U.S. domestic public agenda of the 1960s with that of the late 1970s and early 1980s to reinforce this impression. In the context of fiscal stringency, the productive efficiency of service delivery gains a more prominent role as a social criterion with which to judge the relative performance of sectors and organizations. Simply put, people become more interested in the question of which organizations will deliver service for the least cost. This efficiency criterion is hard to divorce from the trust issue, however. In particular, efficiency can only be referenced with respect to a given level of quality. Thus a trustworthy institution that maintains quality cannot necessarily be said to be less efficient than a less costly agency that depreciates the quality of its services. Nonetheless, microeconomists typically argue that (presumably less trustworthy) proprietary agencies tend to be more efficient because the maximization of profits requires minimization of costs (exclusive of profits) for any given level of quality and output. Overall, therefore, any comparison of productive efficiency by sector, that is, the cost per unit of service of a given quality, must recognize the subtle distinctions among inefficiency, quality depreciation, and profit taking. A commonly held view is that nonprofits maintain quality but produce services in a relatively wasteful fashion, whereas proprietaries produce efficient services of perhaps questionable quality and extract some of the surpluses through profit taking.

Innovation. Chapter 3 reviewed the relationship and the distinction between entrepreneurial activity and innovation and noted that, although technical innovation and invention are not synonymous with entrepreneurship, new ideas, technical methods, and implementation of advanced concepts often form a substantial part of the basis for enterprising behavior. Innovation is a rather indirect social criterion; its relevance pertains more to its contributions to the three previous criteria than as a goal in itself. Innovation may be seen to contribute primarily to efficiency, as new methods or procedures enable agencies to deliver particular services at lower cost or higher quality. Innovation may also contribute to responsiveness in the sense that new technologies may lead to wholly new services, permitting agencies to address unserved or poorly served societal needs or clients. The diagnostic-center concept in child-welfare services provides an example. A much less direct connection exists between innovation and trustworthiness, a link that involves the subtle distinction between innovations that are useful and those that might simply be interesting or more attractive to service producers than to consumers. For example, certain innovations might have great intellectual value to entrepreneurs trained in a particular profession but have uncertain or limited immediate relevance to the needs of constituents. Basic research projects often have this character, although they may proceed in the belief that practical applications will ultimately result. In any case, a trustworthy agency would change on the basis of new ideas clearly relevant to client needs, whereas a less trustworthy agency's concerns would center on innovation for the sake of advancing knowledge in a more abstract sense.

Modes of Behavior

The main strategy of analysis in this book is to develop the sectoral implications of alternative kinds of entrepreneurial motivation. The behavior patterns of each entrepreneurial type will therefore be assessed relative to the four social-performance criteria just considered. This discussion will briefly summarize the behavior patterns of the different entrepreneurial characters developed in earlier chapters and proceed with the social-performance implications of allowing each of these entrepreneurial types to operate freely in the nonprofit sector, only weakly restrained by governmental or constituent machinery of regulation and accountability. Subsequently, the question of how alternative policy instruments that influence the screening and policing of nonprofit agencies result in various mixes and intensities of these social-performance patterns will be considered.

Independent Behavior. Sectors in which the independent variety of entrepreneur is allowed to operate freely would feature the promulgation of multiple, autonomous organizational units, each relatively resistant to external demands or to the internal sharing of authority. Such sectors would respond to external opportunities to fund new ventures leading to the establishment of new units, but existing units established by independents could not be expected to undertake large risks or expansions or to strike out dramatically in new directions. Rather, ventures undertaken in a sector featuring independents will tend to be stable, with dependable, long-term leadership. Thus a new field open to independents or an old field featuring large organizations that is suddenly opened to the independent-minded entrepreneur (for example, through loosened entry controls) would be initially dynamic, featuring the founding of many new organizational units. An older field already saturated with independent-led agencies would tend to be insular and stagnant.

In terms of the four social criteria, sectors that feature independent behavior would tend to be (1) trustworthy in the sense that entrepreneurs will protect their reputations in order to stay in business and jealously guard their autonomy. They will thus avoid false advertising or quality depreciation unless threatened with financial collapse. (2) Responsive in the short-run process of establishing new agencies according to existing social opportunities, but relatively unresponsive (insular) in the long run, once an array of independent agencies is established and entry becomes difficult. (3) Efficient in the sense that costs will be contained to make ends meet. Fraud will be avoided, but no particular incentives to minimize costs or introduce new methods will be demonstrated. Economies deriving from large-scale or interagency cooperation will be specifically forgone. (4) Innovative at the stage of new-agency formation if a new idea is helpful for garnering support to get started. No particular innovative bent will be demonstrated thereafter.

Believer Behavior. Sectors in which believers are given free rein will feature the proliferation of organizations based on single-minded, conscientious pursuit of different (self-defined) causes. Such sectors may exhibit the pursuit of radical ideas and risk-taking behavior stemming from indifference to economic, legal, and personal consequences. Instability from risk taking and conflict with the establishment will be compensated to some extent by dependability that stems from the long-term consistency of purpose, dedication, and commitment of entrepreneurs. The mission of ventures driven by believers will initially be inspired by and derive sustenance from extant social turmoil. Once established, however, believer-based ventures will be internally self-guiding and relatively insensitive to changes in the social context or the demand for services. Change in believer-based sectors basically arises from the establishment of new agencies rather than changing the purposes of old ones. Some believer-based organizations may grow fairly large, but most are limited by the difficulty of believers to delegate authority or share control with others whose ideas might not conform to their own.

In reference to social-performance criteria, believer-oriented nonprofit sectors would tend to be (1) trustworthy in the sense that believers will be true to their stated purposes and will work tirelessly in the cause of advertised goals. The believer-based sector will be selfless rather than self-aggrandizing or fraudulent. (2) Responsive only in the sense that believers have to tap into latent pockets of demand to support their efforts. Believer-based causes are basically self-defined, may be coincident with certain social concerns in the short run, but will be essentially unresponsive to societal pressures in the long run. Agencies led by believers follow an inner calling rather than signals from the outside. (3) Efficient in the sense that resources will be devoted to articulated purposes and waste and fraud will be minimized. Potential economies of scale and interagency cooperation are likely to be passed by because of the basic antagonisms that believers are likely to encounter in working in larger contexts. In addition, as idea and program advocates rather than entrepreneurs with managerial interests, believers may not administer their operations well. (4) Innovative only in the sense that preconceived methods or beliefs represent actual breakthroughs or productive changes in accepted procedure. Strong entrepreneurial support for some causes (for example, research on birth defects) may encourage innovation, however.

Professional Behavior. Sectors in which professional-type entrepreneurs operate freely will tend to feature the proliferation of experimental, demonstration, or show case programs that reflect new ideas under discussion by the relevant discipline. Such a sector is likely to be trendy, perhaps even capricious in its efforts to remain professionally avant-garde. Services of such a sector will tend to be costly, of high quality, and coupled with machinery to document, analyze, and disseminate results. Programs will be designed to be small, and in some scientifically oriented professional contexts, carefully controlled. Generation and distribution of knowledge will be an expressed purpose, but expansion of successful programs will not be enthusiastically undertaken.

Although professional-based agencies act to maintain themselves at the forefront of knowledge generation and disciplinary visibility, they will rarely jeopardize their agencies with ventures of high economic risk or ventures that radically depart from the mainstream of current disciplinary thought. Nor will the professional-based agency continue to nurture programs (past ventures) that are conventional or out of date in the eyes of the discipline.

With reference to the criteria of social performance, professional-based nonprofit sectors will be (1) trustworthy in the sense of delivering services of high quality, with high costs and possible extravagance, but little outright fraud. Services will be delivered as advertised because alleged deception can be professionally damaging. Professional-based agencies cannot be counted on to sustain given service modes for an indefinite period of time, once those modes become conventional. (2) Responsive only in the sense that disciplinary thinking may follow (or even anticipate) developing social problems. New ventures may be designed to alleviate or otherwise address accumulating needs, but a professional-based sector will be unresponsive in terms of providing new services in quantity or in providing conventional, routine services that, although needed, have no special disciplinary interest or appeal. (3) Efficient only in the sense of avoiding outright fraud. Otherwise, there will be little effort in professional-based sectors to produce given varieties of services at minimum cost or to manage ventures in a Spartan manner. Furthermore, professional-based sectors may tend to duplicate variations of trendy experimental programs, and because such programs tend to be small and possibly experimentally controlled and there may be rivalry among alternative professional-based agencies, possible economies of cooperation and scale may be forfeited. (4) Innovative in the sense that professional-based agencies will operate programs at the forefront of disciplinary knowledge, putting new ideas into limited, tentative practice. Although this can be a major source of sectoral change, professional-based agencies will tend to ignore innovations that require cross-disciplinary cooperation and will specifically avoid maverick ideas and methods that run counter to prevailing disciplinary thought or challenge the appropriateness of the discipline itself.

Conserver Behavior. Sectors in which conservers are provided the opportunity to operate freely as entrepreneurial agents will exhibit a strong sense of stability in purpose but may prove to be too rigid or cautious to withstand dramatic changes in the economy or in society at large. Such sectors will protect the character and viability of their existing agencies, adjusting their structures and programs only when threatened by crises, and even then only on an incremental basis. Conserver-based sectors will be averse to ventures that involve large uncertainties and risks, but can be depended on to see ventures through into the indefinite future.

In terms of the social-performance criteria, conserver-based sectors will be (1) trustworthy in the sense of being sensitive to preserving the reputation of cherished institutions. Thus fraudulent or deceptive practices will be avoided, and long-term commitment to stated objectives and promised services may be relied on. (2) Responsiveness in the sense that conserver-based agencies will attempt to adjust their programs and services to avoid major collapse. Otherwise such agencies will attempt to maintain a traditional course, relatively unaffected by environmental changes in demand. (3) Efficient only in the sense that explicit fraud, which may tarnish institutional reputations, will be avoided. Otherwise, management practices will tend to become stagnant, except when jarred and revamped in times of crisis. (4) Innovative only in minor ways that may assist incremental adaptation to new circumstances in times of extreme difficulty.

Architectural Behavior. Nonprofit sectors that afford architect-type entrepreneurs free rein will have an expansionist flavor characterized by opportunistic adaptation to environmental demands as well as long-term commitment to maintaining the viability of individual ventures. Quality will be

maintained as a matter of pride in workmanship and entrepreneurial identification with product. Agencies in the architect-driven mode will be insular
in the sense of preferring to build from within rather than acquire programs
or enter joint or cooperative ventures with other agencies.

Relative to the four social-performance criteria, architect-based sectors
will be (1) trustworthy in the sense of quality maintenance that derives from
inherent pride in workmanship. Commitment to original or advertised
purposes is tenuous, however, depending on how the opportunity structure
for acquiring resources to build shifts over time. (2) Responsive in the sense
that architect-based agencies will explore, in opportunistic fashion, all
available resources for further building, expansion, modification, and tinkering with programs, without strong reference to preconceived directions
or purposes. Thus agencies in architect-based sectors remain sensitive to
changes in demands as expressed in the marketplace, philanthropic quar-
ters, and government funding. (3) Efficient in the sense that architects want
to perfect their mechanisms and have them run smoothly. Expansionary
tendencies will allow exploitation of scale economies but may also lead to
overbuilding (that is, incur diseconomies of scale) if entrepreneurs are
extraordinarily successful in garnering resources. Need for personal identification by entrepreneurs of architectural agencies may forfeit opportunities
for savings through cooperative efforts with other agencies. (4) Innovative
in the sense that architect entrepreneurs will constantly try new administrative or programmatic ideas, components, and structures. Ventures will
exhibit a bigger and different quality, they may be inventive, clever, and
impressive, even tied to a grand organizational design or master plan, but
still mechanical and adaptive rather than derived from an overriding programmatic concept or philosophic principle of service delivery.

Poetic Behavior. Nonprofit sectors that allow unrestrained operation of
poet-type entrepreneurs will be quixotic, featuring multifaceted deploy-
ment of imaginative, wide-ranging, vista-expanding programs. Such sectors
will experience instability associated with risk taking in path-breaking new
ventures and the short time during which poetic entrepreneurs remain
committed to nurturing particular projects. Ventures in sectors of this kind
may involve sweeping changes or small-scale demonstrations of new concepts, undertaken within the confines of an agency on which the poet
entrepreneur singularly imposes his signature. In such sectors, the ideas that
underlie new ventures will be stressed, with the nuts-and-bolts mechanics
given secondary attention. On the four social criteria, the poet-based nonprofit sector will be (1) trustworthy in the sense that entrepreneurs will be
sincere, truthful, and indeed provocative in their intentions. Short attention
spans and disinterest in details, however, may result in service delivery that
falls short of original promises. (2) Responsive in the sense that entrepre-

neurs may seek to solve festering social or other problems through the application of bold new ideas and concepts. Ideas will be pursued more on the basis of intellectual arguments and creative inspiration than direct pressures from the environment, however, and the poet-driven agency will not be readily responsive to demands for implementation or expansion of routine or conventional programs. (3) Efficient in the sense that dynamism at the entrepreneurial level translates into general agitation and questioning of purpose and performance at the operating level. Otherwise, the entrepreneurial preoccupation with expression of new ideas and concepts and lack of attention to operating details and routine operations can lead to various forms of inefficiency, including poor administration and coordination of diverse programs, failure to expand to take advantage of scale economies, and failure to engage in economical cooperative efforts with other agencies. (4) Innovative in the sense that entrepreneurs are constantly preoccupied with new ideas and experiences and will tend to channel these energies into unique projects and programs.

Player Behavior. Sectors in which the player variety of power-seeking entrepreneur is allowed to operate unrestrained will feature increasing concentrations of industrial activity within a relatively few, large, growing, hierarchical organizations. Such a sector will be eager to expand into new areas and to adapt existing services to larger markets. Ventures may lack long-run stability because of the limited time frames of entrepreneurial commitments, and long-term managerial control may be hampered by organizational size and disinterest of entrepreneurs in routine administration.

With respect to social-performance criteria, a player-dominated sector will be (1) trustworthy only to the degree that entrepreneurs fear for their reputations and may be harmed by scandal that would prevent their further advance. Beyond this concern, such sectors will be opportunistic, seeking to divert resources toward visible, attention-garnering activities and shifting policies and service characteristics to suit the moment. Maintenance of quality and fulfillment of advertised service characteristics may therefore prove problematic. (2) Responsive in exhibiting great sensitivity to current issues on the public agenda and ventures that can attract immediate support. Agencies in player-based sectors will therefore be highly adaptive to demands for new services by government agencies or shifts of economic resources that allow new consumer groups to express their demands in a tangible manner. (3) Efficient in that economies of scale will be exploited and opportunities for merger and consolidation of weaker programs will be pursued. However, player-led organizations can become inefficient in the sense that programs may grow too large and uncontrollable or they may be poorly administered. Furthermore, resources may be diverted for self-serving purposes, including top-heavy staffing, perquisites of office that signify prestige, and programs that have glamor and visibility but low productivity. (4) Innovative in the sense that player-based agencies will latch on to new ideas that have significant resource-producing or publicity-producing potentials. However, risks associated with the implementation of innovations will be carefully calculated, and innovations are unlikely to be undertaken unless they have been tried elsewhere and will not antagonize large groups of people.

Controller Behavior. Controller-dominated sectors will exhibit behavior patterns reminiscent of both the independent and player modes. Ventures will be aimed at expanding existing agencies within limits of the entrepreneur's ability to retain effective central control. Within self-imposed growth limits, agencies will respond opportunistically to changes in the demand environment to increase resources and staff. Controller-based organizations will be more conservatively run and more meticulously managed than player-based ones and larger and more outward looking than independent-based agencies.

With respect to the four social criteria, agencies in controller-based sectors will be (1) trustworthy to the degree that entrepreneurs fear that their power and control may be shaken by scandal, misrepresentation, or depreciation of quality. (2) Responsive in the sense that opportunities to garner additional resources for new or expanded programs will be sought as a way of increasing entrepreneurial power within limits of controllability. Thus controller-based agencies will be relatively adaptive to changing demands of government agencies and markets. (3) Efficient to the degree that retention of effective control requires meticulous management, and the limits of controllability also allow exploitation of economies of scale. Inefficiency may result from the reluctance of entrepreneurs to enter beneficial cooperative ventures with other agencies (which dilutes their control) and from the possible overdiversion of resources to top-level staff, which allows entrepreneurs to monitor their organizations more closely and to experience power from the control of the staff. (4) Innovative in the same sense in which player-based agencies are innovative, that is, in the adoption of relatively new ideas that attract resources to permit agencies to expand within desired limits.

Income-Seeking Behavior. Nonprofit sectors in which income seekers have free rein will exhibit a strongly opportunistic pattern of development, highly adaptive to current social priorities as expressed through economic demands of government, private consumers, or third parties. Opportunities for quality depreciation and fraud will be exploited where consumers or funding agents cannot maintain vigilance and cost-cutting savings can be diverted to salaries or other modes of personal wealth augmentation. Income seeker-based nonprofits will, in effect, act like profit maximizers—raising prices (padding reimbursable costs) and expanding output to maximize the difference between revenues and minimum costs—except that profits will appear as additional components of expenditure. Thus, in a highly disaggregated income-seeking sector, output levels and prices may be optimal if competitive pressures are allowed to operate. However, in more concentrated sectors or where agencies in disaggregated sectors can collude, output is likely to be restricted and prices kept artificially high, as in a monopolistic profit-making industry. Ventures in income-seeker-based sectors will experience instability insofar as market demands for services are volatile and entrepreneurs' attentions are diverted from one profitable venture to the next.

With respect to the four social-performance criteria, income-seeker-based nonprofit sectors are (1) trustworthy only insofar as consumers and other resource providers are vigilant and able to exert their influence through choice of suppliers or other (regulatory) means. Otherwise, organizations in such sectors present a risk of quality depreciation, fraud, profiteering, and misrepresentation of promised services. (2) Responsive to demands for new services or expansion of existing services as long as these demands are expressed through willingness-to-pay levels that can provide revenues in excess of minimum costs. Highly concentrated or collusive sectors may raise prices and restrict output short of socially optimal levels. (3) Efficient in the sense that inherently wasteful (costly) methods of operation will be avoided, but inefficient because components of costs that can be effectively drawn out as entrepreneurial profits will be artifically inflated. (4) Innovative where new methods are able to lower minimum costs or attract new sources of demand. When possible innovations promise an uncertain return, calculated risks will be taken.

Searcher Behavior. Nonprofit sectors that give free rein to searchers are likely to be in newly defined fields or in variations of established industries that have not been claimed as the domains of particular professions or disciplines. The principal mode of venture response will be the establishment of new agencies rather than program development within existing agencies. Searchers will tend to identify latent coalitions of supporters and resource providers (new government funding programs, pockets of unserved constituents groups) that form the potential basis for starting new services. In this sense, searcher-based sectors are opportunistic, with enterprise founded on identifying the sources of latent demand and incipient service trends rather than on self-defined or independently conceived ideas or beliefs. Because of entrepreneurial inexperience, uncertainty of personal goals, and the novel character of ventures, searcher-based sectors are likely to exhibit instability and tenuousness in the nature of ventures.

With respect to the criteria of social performance, searcher-based non-profit sectors will be (1) trustworthy in that entrepreneurs, operating out of conscience and frustration, are legitimately seeking to provide services that they feel are useful and required. Furthermore, because they face the uphill tasks of establishing themselves in new areas, entrepreneurs will be sensitive to reputation, wishing to avoid scandals that could result from fraud or misrepresentation. (2) Responsive in the sense that entrepreneurs will seek out the nooks and crannies of latent demand and newly emerging areas of funding and try to develop and implement them. Although searchers may be highly selective of the kinds of activities in which they become involved, they will also tend to develop areas that are neglected by other entrepreneurial types. (3) Efficient in that searchers, at least initially, will have to scrape by and make do with the minimal resources available to new fields that require definition, justification, and focusing. Such sectors are also potentially inefficient, as entrepreneurs may lack management skills, experience, or access to tested methods. (4) Innovative more by necessity than design. The seeking out and development of new service areas is likely to require the formulation of new methods and procedures.

Review

Table 10–1 provides an approximate summary of the performance character of nonprofit sectors in which the various types of entrepreneurs are allowed to operate freely. In general, it is noteworthy that compromises or trade-offs among the four criteria appear to be an inherent necessity. That is, assuming that the postulated set of motivations are relatively complete and that perfect policing or molding of behavior through regulatory means is impossible, then behavior derived from the screening of entrepreneurs into a given sector will necessarily come up short on at least one social criterion. The main trade-off seems to occur between trustworthiness and responsiveness, with strong positive correlations between responsiveness, efficiency, and innovation. As a result, the entrepreneurial types appear to separate roughly into two categories: the trustworthy types and the innovative, efficient, responsive types. The first group includes independents, believers, professionals, and conservers. The second group includes players, controllers, architects, and income seekers. Poets and searchers have some of the positive attributes of each group.

The key question for policy is what effects various policy instruments can be expected to have on the screening and postscreening discretionary behavior of the various types of entrepreneurial characters, and hence on the performance of the sectors within which they operate. The following discussion will focus on a number of policy proposals often considered in

Table 10–1
Social-Performance Criteria and Entrepreneurial Behavior

Behavior Mode	Trust	Response	Efficiency	Innovation
Independent	Positive	Short-run positive; long-run negative	Neutral to negative	Neutral
Believer	Positive	Neutral	Neutral	Neutral
Professional	Positive	Negative	Negative	Positive
Conserver	Positive	Negative	Neutral	Negative
Architect	Neutral	Positive	Neutral to positive	Positive
Poet	Positive	Neutral	Neutral to negative	Positive
Player	Negative	Positive	Neutral to negative	Positive
Controller	Neutral to negative	Positive	Positive	Positive
Income Seeker	Negative	Positive	Neutral to positive	Positive
Searcher	Positive	Positive	Neutral	Positive

connection with delivery of services in industries that involve nonprofit participation. The concern here is how such policy instruments affect behavior and performance within the nonprofit sector and, additionally, in service-producing industries as a whole.

Policy Instruments

The analysis of sector-level screening in chapter 7 suggested that nonprofit sectors tend to draw primarily on the believer, conserver, poet, searcher, and professional varieties of entrepreneur. This entrepreneurial mix leans decidedly toward the trustworthy category and away from the responsive category of performance identified above. However, this tentative conclusion is contingent on the assumptions that (a) selection at the industry level is not heavily biased toward or against any particular type of entrepreneur; (b) the nonprofit sector in the industry in question follows the general pattern of income potential, bureaucratic structure, and service ethic presumed to be characteristic of nonprofit sectors; and (c) the opportunity structures for employment are open enough to allow latent entrepreneurs relatively unconstrained sector selection.

Clearly, industries vary considerably on these conditions; thus the behavioral mixes of alternative nonprofit sectors also vary. Rather than dwell on a behavior mix that may characterize a nominal, hypothetical nonprofit sector, it will be more analytically useful and relevant to consider the implications of variations in these conditions, particularly as these variations are brought about by public policies addressed to the role of nonprofit organizations in specific industries that deliver essential services.

In response to public concerns over the quality of services or the integrity with which essential services are delivered, policies intended to specifically delimit and regulate the kinds of agencies or people that may practice in a given area of economic activity have often been proposed and frequently implemented. Four such policies commonly encountered are (1) the requirement that service-delivery organizations be incorporated as nonprofit; (2) the requirement that practitioners be qualified members of a particular profession or discipline; (3) the control of entry of new agencies into an industry or into the nonprofit sector of that industry; and (4) the targeting to nonprofit agencies of resource commitments of government funding programs. Such policies are intended to increase the trustworthiness or the competence of service providers by attempting to exclude or control undesirable individuals or organizations. As implied in chapters 6, 7, and 8, such policies may affect the screening of entrepreneurial motivations into alternative sectors and industries over the long run and may affect discretionary behavior of those already screened in the short run. Performance implications for industries and their nonprofit sectors, often different from those anticipated by policy designers, may be seen to flow from these effects.

Nonprofitization. Distrust of the profit motive is the main motivating element for those who have proposed the elimination of proprietary interests and the concentration on nonprofit agencies as primary vehicles for the delivery of social, health, educational, and other varieties of essential services. Vladeck's perspective from the nursing-home industry reflects the general picture.

> Expansion of nonprofit ownership is seen by some observers as the only way to improve the nursing home industry. They see for-profit ownership as the original sin at the root of many of the industry's problems because of the inherent conflict between the provision of high quality services to the dependent elderly and profit maximization. As most other kinds of health care institutions are operated on a not-for-profit basis with apparently happy results, public health professionals tend to be made uneasy by profit-seeking firms. So it is not surprising that a number of studies of the nursing home industry have concluded with calls for eliminating proprietary interests and, though formal limitations on proprietary ownership have not been adopted in any state, the trend toward slowly increasing market share for the voluntaries continues. Policymakers have sought to limit the spread of proprietary interests to other areas of health care, most notably to the provision of home health services.[9]

To a lesser extent, nonprofitization initiatives are also intended to remove government as a direct service supplier, for example, by substituting purchase-of-service arrangements with private or independent nonprofit organizations. Various arguments, including the alleged inefficiency of direct government supply and improvement in the flexibility and accountability in use of government funds when the government finance function is separated from the production task, have been made on behalf of such arrangements.[10] The following discussion thus considers nonprofitization a policy of confining an industry solely to private, nonprofit organizational participants.

A policy that requires all agencies in a particular industry to become nonprofit can be expected to have both short-run and long-run effects.

In the short run, imposition of a nonprofitization policy will bring into the nonprofit sector those entrepreneurs who have previously screened themselves into the proprietary and public sectors of the given industry. This result follows from the initial effects of screening discussed in chapter 7: once entrepreneurs have been screened into industries and into particular organizations, they will tend to remain in those positions, even if this requires conversion to nonprofit status. Such conversion, however, conflicts with entrepreneurs' sector-related preferences for income, bureaucratic structure, and service ethic, leading to various patterns of behavior subversive to the character of the nonprofit sector. This conversion also changes the basic behavioral mix within that sector.

Alternatively, a product-differentiation tactic may be taken by some entrepreneurs who wish to avoid conversion to nonprofit status. New industries may be defined in an effort to circumvent the nonprofitization edict. For example, proprietary child-care facilities may be relabeled as residential schools or mental-health treatment centers if the latter are not covered by the nonprofitization policy and if alternative means of support can be found outside the set of resources normally reserved for the industry as originally defined.

In the long run, a nonprofitization policy will cause changes in the patterns of screening for latent entrepreneurs entering the industry. In particular, a nonprofitization policy may, over time, affect the industrial structure (concentration and size of organizations) as well as access to the (material, power) rewards associated with the industry's social priority—variables on which latent entrepreneurs make career decisions. As a result, certain types of entrepreneurs who might previously have selected the industry may screen themselves elsewhere. Over time, the increased heterogeneity of motives in the nonprofit sector and the mismatches of motives that inspire subversive behavior induced by nonprofitization in the short run are likely to decline. They will not disappear, however, because industry-screening decisions are made on other grounds as well as on industrial structure and social priority (for example, nature of service and professional control) and tend to dominate the issue of sector selection within industries.

The particular behavioral implications of a nonprofitization policy on a given industry can be discerned by reviewing each entrepreneurial type, using as a base the nominal screening pattern of figure 7–1.

Income seekers and independents, likely to have been previously screened into the proprietary sector, will in the short run be brought into the nonprofit sector. In the long run, some future entrepreneurs of these types may choose other industries.

Power seekers, especially players, likely to have been previously screened into the public sector, will in the short run be brought into the nonprofit sector. In the long run, some future entrepreneurs of this kind may also select other industries.

Because, believers, professionals, conservers, artists, and searchers will tend to concentrate in the nonprofit sector to begin with, no major shifts of these types may occur from a policy of nonprofitization. However, particular industries vary considerably on this score. For example, in some industries, such as scientific research, the proprietary sector may have created conditions especially conducive to professionals or to architects. In such cases, these types would also exhibit similar short-run and long-run shifts under a nonprofitization policy.

The main implications for behavior and performance within the non-profit sector of these screening shifts may be described as a combination of the following developments.

Income-seeking behavior would become more intense, and the non-distribution constraint would be more sorely tested. The nonprofit sector would become less trustworthy, featuring increased incidence of indirect profiteering and fraud. The sector would also become more responsive to societal demands as expressed through the marketplace and government funding programs.

Autonomy-seeking behavior would increase, leading to entry of new agencies or decentralization and fragmentation of existing agencies, depending on the stringency of entry controls. In the short run, this situation would represent an increase in responsiveness, but in the long run such responsiveness would be retarded by the conservative bent of established independents.

Assuming that governmental provision is also precluded by nonprofit-ization, the responsiveness of the nonprofit sector would be increased by the entry of power seekers, and the trustworthiness of that sector would be decreased for the same reason. Depending on the balance between the decentralizing tendencies of independent types and the centralizing inclinations of power seekers, the nonprofit sector could become either more or less concentrated than it would be in the absence of a nonprofitization policy.

It is interesting to reflect on how the prior implications of the analysis compare with the intentions and expectations of those who propose a policy of nonprofitization. Clearly the designers of such policies have in mind increasing the trustworthiness of services. According to the analysis here, some of the less trustworthy motivational types may indeed, in the long run, drop out of the industry, and entrepreneurs of those types who are shifted into the nonprofit sector (by force in the short run and by selection in the long run) may find it more difficult to carry out their objectives in the nonprofit domain, although the intensity of this effect depends on how well nonprofit regulations are policed.

On the other hand, a policy of nonprofitization may stimulate new labels and variations of service outside the nonprofit sector according to the product-differentiation effect noted above. To the degree that such differentiated services are able to retain or attract new resources (from the marketplace or alternative government programs), the nonprofitization policy will be limited in its potential for improving the trustworthy character of the industry as a whole. Overall, however, some industry-wide improvement in trustworthiness may be anticipated, although probably much less than policy proponents would argue.

Whatever the net result on industries as a whole, it is clear that nonprofitization will have a corrupting influence on the nonprofit sector, making it less pure and less easily describable in terms of particular motivations and modes of behavior and performance. Thus a nonprofitizaton policy may be expected to improve industry-level performance but also to obfuscate the character and trustworthiness of the nonprofit sector.

Entry Controls. Varying degrees of difficulty are associated with the founding of a new agency in the nonprofit sector. In some areas, such as management consulting, establishing a nonprofit may be as simple as filing a few papers and paying an incorporation fee. In other areas, stringent need and necessity standards may be imposed by regulatory bodies or heavy capital investments may be necessary. In some fields, such as nursing-home and health services, the use of entry controls has increased over time and is likely to become even more prominent.[11]

Entry-control policies allow state agencies to restrict the formation of new agencies directly through the manipulation of approvals, and indirectly, by increasing the costs of surmounting the entry process and meeting the imposed standards of operation. Furthermore, such controls may limit the growth and development of programs within established organizations. Although such controls may apply to programs of existing agencies, the most severe effects are felt by would-be entrants from the outside who normally have fewer resources and less expertise for negotiating the system.

Entry controls may apply evenly to an industry as a whole, or they may be differentially severe toward one or more sectors within an industry. In some cases, controls on entry have been observed to favor the nonprofit sector—in broadcasting, for example, where a certain portion of licenses have been reserved for educational radio and television,[12] and in higher education, where accrediting bodies have rejected applications by proprietary institutions.[13] In such cases, the effects of entry control are similar to those of a nonprofitization policy, though perhaps less severe.

Entry-control polices may also discriminate against nonprofits. The process of incorporation, itself a form of entry control, can be especially difficult for novice nonprofit applicants, especially as such groups are required to clarify their public purposes, prove their ties to the community, and demonstrate financial viability. Application for tax-exempt status can be similarly arduous.

Even a nominally uniform policy of entry control across an industry may discriminate against nonprofits, because fledgling nonprofits will be implicitly handicapped in their abilities to raise capital or to put together the necessary coalitions of community sponsors.[14] Hence they will be slower to apply for the available spaces in an industry, the number of which is limited by entry control.

The following analysis supposes that entry controls would be relatively more severe for the nonprofit sector than elsewhere, but effective only in limiting entry of new organizations rather than new programs of established agencies.

Entry controls with a more severe impact on the nonprofit sector of given industry would have the following short-run and long-run effects.

In the short run, entry controls would cause mismatches of (sector-related) preferences for those entrepreneurial types already screened into the nonprofit sector but who favor small agencies or the option of forming new agencies. Such entrepreneurs would be locked into the nonprofit sector by the inertial tendencies of the sector-screening process. Entry control would cause them to operate at diminished levels of activity, but also to undertake ventures that subvert the design of this policy. Entry controls may also liberate the energies of those entrepreneurs already screened into the nonprofit sector, whose preferences center on power and concentration of activity.

In the long run, screening effects will attract to the nonprofit sector future entrepreneurs who prefer the greater concentrations of economic activity induced by entry control and will divert those entrepreneurial types who prefer more decentralized regimes.

Independents who may have been screened into the nonprofit sector will find themselves bound to that sector (and particular organization) by inertial tendencies and also inhibited in their proclivity to venture by the imposition of entry controls. Nonetheless, they may attempt to venture from within their agencies, that is, to promote decentralization of their agencies and set up autonomous enclaves internally. In the long run, however, future independent types will be discouraged by entry controls from entering employment in the nonprofit sector. `

Power seekers previously screened into the nonprofit sector may pursue their ventures with renewed vigor after imposition of entry controls. In the long run, future power-seeking entrepreneurs will be more strongly attracted to the nonprofit sector as a result of this policy.

Searchers who might otherwise consider the nonprofit sector for its venture possibilities will in the long run (process of screening) direct their explorations elsewhere as a result of restricted entry policy.

Other types of entrepreneurs are less likely than independents, power seekers, or searchers to be seriously affected in their short-run behavior or screening tendencies by an entry-control policy. Some, like the architect, professional, income seeker, or conserver, will be relatively indifferent, and others, like the poet and believer, will be antagonistic but unlikely to change their sectoral preferences. However, the latter two types may emulate the short-term behavior of the independent in his attempts to decentralize existing organizational structures.

Note that, generally speaking, these effects are likely to be relatively weak. In the case of independents and power seekers, for example, the entrepreneurs would already be predisposed toward other sectors and may not be found in the nonprofit sector in great numbers to begin with. In the case of independents, entry controls would simply reinforce the screening tendencies otherwise at work; and such controls may not change the bureaucratic structure of the nonprofit sector enough to attract large numbers of power seekers from the public sector. To the extent that entry restriction does induce observable effects, corresponding behavior and performance implications may be expected.

The nonprofit sector will tend to become more concentrated and subject to power-seeking behavior, especially in the long run, with entrepreneurial activity taking place by internal expansion of existing organizations rather than formation of new ones. Some decentralization within those agencies may be observed, however, via (short-run) activity of independents. The loss of searchers and independents and the gain of power seekers may yield little net change on the responsiveness dimension, but a net loss in trustworthiness.

The nominal intended purposes of entry control in nonprofit sectors is certainly at odds with the foregoing analysis. Indeed, entry restrictions are usualiy imposed in an attempt to screen out, or at least restrain, untrustworthy elements. Thus the expected direction, if not intensity, of the predicted effects does not appear to support entry restriction as a productive policy.

Professionalization. A trend toward increased and more specialized training and licensing of key personnel has pervaded almost the entire spectrum of services in which nonprofit provision is an important part. Through the decades of this century, the education, health, social-work, fine-arts, and research fields have all explicitly or implicitly imposed and reinforced stringent requirements for licensing practitioners and, by extension, for requiring professional credentials of managerial and entrepreneurial personnel. A similar policy thrust is often proposed for emerging service areas, such as preschool and day-care services for children and nursing-home care for the elderly. Although the nominal intent of a professionalization policy is to increase the competence and integrity of service providers, such proposals are not viewed with unanimous or unqualified enthusiam. As Vladeck explains, in the case of nursing homes inflation is one fear, as professionals are trained and ethically constrained to assure the highest possible service quality without regard to cost.[15]

Other concerns are raised by pursuing the analysis of screening and discretionary behavior. A policy that requires entrepreneurial personnel in a given industry to qualify as professionals of a particular educational discipline (for example, social work, education, medicine, art, or music) may affect the motivational structure of nonprofit sectors in a number of ways. Alternative disciplines—by reinforcing the social, technical, or creative character of services—were seen in chapter 7 to encourage different motivational traits. Furthermore, the various professions were observed to filter candidates on the basis of ethical values bearing on material reward and power seeking. Whatever the particular motivational biases introduced by a given discipline, the control of an industry by a certain profession—through processes of certification of personnel—will have two principal effects.

In the short run, professionalization will tend to suffocate entrepreneurial activity by those without the relevant training, but it may also encourage product differentiation through ventures operating parallel to, but technically outside, the industry. Specifically, previously screened entrepreneurs, unqualified by new disciplinary standards but locked into careers by postscreening inertia, may attempt to circumvent the professionalization policy by redefining their activities as different industries. This situation is similar to that observed under nonprofitization.

In the long run, professionalization will tend to narrow the distribution of entrepreneurship in the industry, by screening out those motivational types inconsistent with the values promoted by the professional discipline and attracting more strongly those with compatible interests.

The short-run effect results from the fact that professionalization, coupled with rigorous standards or degree requirements for qualification in the discipline, will effectively exclude some entrepreneurs who are committed to a particular field, for example, those engaged in child care but without a master's degree in social work. Such individuals will seek to continue to provide similar services under alternative auspices, for example, through educational institutions or mental-health clinics.

In the long run, as disciplinary control takes hold, fringe movements will tend to be eliminated or overwhelmed as new aspirants to the industry recognize the discipline as the appropriate and accepted entry mode. Aberrations may still occur, however, where whole disciplinary approaches come under attack and entrepreneurs from outside the discipline are able to attract support, for example, the entry of educational-consultant firms into public education during the period of experimentation with performance contracting,[16] where there is controversy within the industry as to appropriate modes of training, for example the desirability of business training for leaders of museums,[17] or where the profession itself creates a vacuum, for example, the successful entrepreneurial entry by non-social-work mavericks into child care, in circumstances where the social-work establishment has failed to mobilize appropriate services for violent children.

The net social-performance effects of professionalization must be considered in two parts—general implications and implications peculiar to particular disciplines.

In the short run and over time, a policy of professionalization will tend to reduce searchers as a source of entrepreneurial energy, because qualifications for disciplinary competence usually require early career decisions and enrollment in appropriate educational curricula. The searcher often lacks such specific training and may be reluctant to make such an investment at his later stage of life. In addition, a policy of professionalization will obviously discourage generalists—those with business, law, or liberal-arts educations. Generalists in a service-producing field are more likely to be income seekers and power seekers, because these motives reflect some of the key reasons that people choose to obtain such flexible, pragmatic training; therefore, a policy of professionalization is likely to weed out these types as well.

Nonetheless, professionalization is also likely to have monopolistic effects—restricting the labor pool and lifting the income potential of those who enter the discipline—thus attracting (properly trained) income seekers, partially nullifying the generalist effect noted above. In addition, the profession itself will create a power structure through which power-seekers (players) can gain influence and fame (through participation in professional associations) within the industry and social arena as a whole. These latter effects, because they are spread thin over the discipline as a whole (that is, income benefits are not concentrated in entrepreneurial hands, and power opportunities in professional associations are relatively few), will tend to moderate but not overwhelm the former effects. Hence, mainly as a result of the loss of income seekers and power seekers, an industry in which a professionalization policy is introduced may be expected to gain somewhat in trustworthiness over the long run but to lose some of its ability to respond to changes in the social demand for services.

Coupled with these general effects, a policy of professionalization will differentially alter the motivational structure in particular industries. For this discussion services will again be divided into three broad categories—social, technical, and creative.

Professions in the socially oriented services stress altruism and social purpose and deemphasize accumulation of personal wealth and power. As a result, a policy of professionalization will cause the industry to differentially attract more believers and poets and to further underrepresent income seekers and powerseekers. Professionalization will thus move a socially oriented industry toward those varieties of entrepreneurial behavior that inspire trustworthiness but may further inhibit responsiveness to changes in social demands for service.

Professions in the creative industries emphasize and reinforce originality and expression of ideas, technical excellence, and human values. A policy of professionalization in such fields will differentially encourage entrepreneurs of the poet, professional, and architect varieties and implicitly discourage other types. This situation leads to relatively neutral or weakly positive effects on trustworthiness and responsiveness, and a net positive effect in terms of the potential for significant methodological or product innovations.

Professions in the technical-service fields will reemphasize technical competence, intellectual honesty, and pecuniary reward as a symbol for achievement and advanced training. Ideological and expressionistic modes of initiative (believers, poets) will be discouraged in favor of intellectual and material modes (professionals and income seekers). In the long run, such a field may lose some of its trustworthiness but exhibit a stronger inclination toward technical innovation. Its responsiveness orientation will be bifurcated—featuring the restraint of professionals and the enthusiasm of income seekers.

Resource Targeting. Many nonprofits operate in industries where government provides operating revenues and capital through grant and contracting programs, fees for services, or other funding arrangements. In addition, government influences the cost of doing business in these industries through its taxation, labor-market, and other policies. Frequently such government programs specifically favor organizations in the nonprofit sector. Indeed Hansmann observes that "Large classes of nonprofits receive special treatment in almost all areas in which federal legislation impinges upon them significantly, including corporate income taxation, Social Security, unemployment insurance, the minimum wage, securities, regulations, . . . and postal rates".[18]

In the health field, Clark cites biases toward nonprofits in the areas of unemployment compensation, taxation, tax deductibility for gifts, grants and loans for health-maintenance organizations, planning grants, terms of reimbursement under Medicare, and property taxation.[19] In communications, Schutzer cites special federal funding for public television and radio stations.[20]

In the performing arts, Netzer observes that the "dominant approach [for funding] in this country . . . is to provide support to nonprofit organizations and individual artists through a government foundation."[21] For federal museum funding, Meyer notes that a "museum" is defined as "a public or private nonprofit agency which is organized on a permanent basis for essentially educational or aesthetic purposes, and which, using a professional staff, owns or uses tangible objects . . . and exhibits them to the public on a regular basis."[22] In the child-care field, reviewed by Young and Finch, federal, state, and local funding for residential care may be essentially restricted to nonprofit providers.[23] Finally, in the field of home-health care, Vladeck cites targeting developments promoted by those who fear a repeat of the recent experience with proprietary nursing homes and would prefer to see the industry develop via the growth of voluntary home-health agencies.[24]

Public funding programs that target resources specifically to nonprofits will have behavioral effects that differ from those of programs that inject funds on an industry-wide basis without regard to sector.

A policy that provides new funds for an industry without discriminating by sector will have the following effects. In the short run, it may differentially stimulate entrepreneurship in those sectors into which certain responsive entrepreneurial types have previously been screened. In the long run, it may cause certain types of entrepreneurs to be screened into the industry and it may alter the distribution of entrepreneurial types among sectors of the industry.

At any point in time, a given industry is likely to have a nonuniform distribution of entrepreneurial types among sectors and these entrepreneurial types are likely to be differentially responsive to new funding opportunities. In the short run, the introduction of a significant new resource program (such as vendor payments for nursing homes) may differentially encourage the response of particular sectors, even though the resource policy is nondiscriminatory. The reason for this situation derives partly from the fact that funding programs are likely to have strings attached that constrain the use of funds to particular program purposes, designs, or service patterns. As a result, entrepreneurs who are concept bound (as noted in chapter 8) will be more inhibited in their responses than those characterized as value free and not bound by a specific ideology or program concept. In short, the more adaptive, value-free types are likely to be first out of the gate.

Income seekers, more likely to be concentrated in the proprietary sector, will react rapidly to expand programs in this sector. This situation has occurred in nursing homes and, according to Vladeck, appears to be under way in homes for adults, through Supplemental Security Income (SSI) financing.[25] Power seekers, more likely to be found in the public sector, will build up programs in that sector.

Architects are somewhat less predictable in their sector affiliations but are likely to be differentially concentrated in the nonprofit or proprietary domains; hence they will stimulate the growth of these sectors when general new funding programs are introduced.

Overall, the less adaptive believers, professionals, poets, and conservers, who tend to concentrate in the nonprofit domain more than elsewhere, will slow that sector's short-run response to the introduction of a major, new, government funding program. Note that this effect may be partially compensated by the efforts of such entrepreneurs to bend funding opportunities to their own programmatic purposes, but such attempts may be expected to be piecemeal and hard to sustain. The handicapping effect of the nonadaptive entrepreneurial types is a matter of degree, however, declining in potency for funding programs that are more flexible in their requirements or more attuned to the particular ideas of one or more of these entrepreneurial types.

In the long run, the short-run results of a nondiscriminatory but constrained funding program are likely to be reinforced through screening. The value-free types of entrepreneurs will be drawn to the industry in greater numbers than the concept-bound types and will be more heavily attracted to the proprietary and public sectors of that industry. Thus the new funding program will attract income seekers, who sense opportunities to increase their wealth; power seekers and architects, who sense the chance to employ public funds as a resource for building organizational structures and power bases; and searchers, if resources are targeted to new service areas yet unmined by established agencies.

Resource programs with looser strings attached may also attract other entrepreneurial characters: independents, if regulatory control and accountability for funding is light-handed and does not intrude on executive decision-making autonomy; professionals, if funded services can be defined in terms consistent with current disciplinary interests; and believers, poets, and conservers, if funding is flexible enough to encompass their individualistic entrepreneurial interests or if there is a fortunate confluence of entrepreneurial and funding-program objectives.

Overall, however, a resource-targeting policy that is nondiscriminatory by sector but retains effective programmatic guidelines on use of funds will lead in the long run to an industry that is more responsive but less trustworthy and that exhibits a relative loss of vigor of the nonprofit sector.

Resource-targeting programs that differentially favor the nonprofit sector may be intended, in part, to compensate for the presumed response handicaps as well as to capitalize on the presumed trustworthiness of that sector. Such a policy may be expected to have substantially different implications than those of a nondiscriminatory policy. A policy that specifically targets resources to the nonprofit part of an industry will in the short run, stimulate venture activity by those entrepreneurial types already screened into the nonprofit sector of the industry. In the long run, such a policy will make the nonprofit sector more heterogeneous in its motivational content by attracting various types of entrepreneurs from other sectors and industries.

The short-run effect follows from the view that, within whatever inhibitions are posed by funding constraints (concept-bound) entrepreneurs in the nonprofit sector will nonetheless respond in some measure to opportunities for venture created by the injection of new resource programs, however much they may have to wrestle to bend the programs to their own designs. Moreover, some value-free entrepreneurial types may have been previously screened into the nonprofit sector as well. Those types will tend to be more vigorous in their response than their concept-bound colleagues, thus skewing the nonprofit sector in the short run toward a more responsive but less trustworthy orientation.

In the long run, funding programs targeted specifically to nonprofits will attract certain types of entrepreneurs to the industry as a whole, and from other sectors to the nonprofit sector in particular. As a consequence, the nonprofit sector will become more heterogeneous in its mix of entrepreneurial motivations. More specifically, such a policy will, like nonprofitization, induce a shift of income seekers and, perhaps, independents from the proprietary sector and a shift of power seekers from the public sector to the nonprofit sector of the industry. Unlike nonprofitization, however, a policy that targets resources to the nonprofit sector will encourage rather than discourage an influx of such types from outside the industry as well. Thus the nonprofit sector will become more heterogeneous, more responsive, and less trustworthy than it would be without such a policy, as will the industry as a whole.

The intent of public funding policies is usually to increase and upgrade the kinds of services produced by a given industry. This analysis implies that injection of resources is likely to stimulate activity by those entrepreneurial types who will tend to make industries more responsive to government-articulated societal needs but less reliable or trustworthy in delivering the services associated with addressing those needs. An across-the-board funding program would appear to maintain the nonprofit sector in a relatively more trustworthy state, but to erode the vigor of that sector relative to others. Alternatively, a policy of targeting resources specifically to nonprofits would tend to make that sector more of a cosmos of all entrepreneurial types—yielding a more heterogeneous, less trustworthy, more responsive sector and a more heterogeneous, responsive, and less trustworthy industry as well.

Policing of Nonprofit Constraints

Earlier discussion has shown that (a) entrepreneurs screened into a non-profit sector may be inclined to engage in various forms of discretionary behavior according to their particular objectives, and (b) the structure of the nonprofit sector itself tends to allow for such discretion. The diffuse nature of performance criteria, the diversity and fragmentation of constituent groups, and the separation of resource allocation from resource accumulation in the nonprofit arena were seen to be responsible for this margin of indulgence. The degree of entrepreneurial discretion is not some fixed, immutable factor, however. One option for the government is to devote increased resources to the policing of regulatory constraints on nonprofits, with the objective of limiting certain forms of discretionary action.

Across industries, the regulatory instruments available to government are numerous and varied, some applying to all organizations within a particular service area and others peculiarly applicable to nonprofits. This section is concerned with the latter. It will focus on three generic types of institutional constraints that specifically apply to nonprofits and that reflect the intended and presumed nature of the nonprofit form, namely, its deemphasis of financial gain, its dedication to public purposes, and its voluntary, cooperative modes of participation and decision making. These three sets of constraints are: (1) fiscal requirements, that is, the nondistribution constraint and rules for tax exemption; (2) requirements for shared decision making between agency executives and boards of directors or trustees; and (3) networking mandates that emphasize public accountability and cooperative programming among nonprofit organizations in a given community or industry.

The effect of enforcement of such requirements on discretionary behavior is considered below. Subsequently, the complementarities that may exist between the implementation of particular public policies—nonprofitization, professionalization, entry control, and resource targeting—and the intensity of policing these nonprofit constraints are considered. The intent here is to see whether coupling these policies with policing can eliminate some of the negative performance implications and retain the benefits of these policies.

Each of the entrepreneurial characters, if unrestrained, will indulge in discretionary excesses of various kinds, including autonomy seeking by independents and controllers, excessive expansion by architects, and pursuit of independent goals by believers, poets, and professionals. Income seekers will look for ways to siphon agency resources for personal use, and players will use agency resources to promote personal visibility or status or to build empires through excessive expansion. The most worrisome form of discretion is the self-aggrandizement of income seekers and players that leads most ostensibly to the losses of trustworthiness associated with implementation of the public policies—nonprofitization, resource targeting, and entry control, in particular—considered above.

Policing of the nonprofit constraints may be seen to potentially impinge on these particular discretionary-behavior modes in various ways.

Enforcement of the nondistribution constraint and tax-exemption rules makes self-aggrandizement more difficult to indulge. For example, within limits, stiffer and more frequent auditing will inhibit the siphoning of resources through obviously inflated salaries, improper arrangements for purchasing input resources, or other fiscal irregularities. Such auditing will also tend to raise questions about legal but questionable practices such as over-intensive staffing, extensive travel, or other unusual concentrations of resources that might reflect personal more than programmatic goals. According to Smith, enforcement of tax-exempt status has the potential for special cogency.

> the tax exempt status of the nonprofit corporation is hardly an automatic and irrevocable right enjoyed by any group wishing to proclaim itself a "nonprofit" organization. Tax-exempt status can be lost if an organization fails to observe defining conditions laid down by law, administrative action, and court decision. The witholding or withdrawal of tax-exempt status gives the federal government a powerful tool to regulate the activities of nonprofit corporations.[26]

In sum, enforcement of the fiscal constraints on nonprofits may help ameliorate discretionary self-enrichment within the nonprofit sector or the use of resources to promote personal visibility or status.

Encouraging shared decision making between agency executives and boards of directors is a policing option in industries in which nonprofit agencies that are recipients of government funds must receive charter or licensing approval or are otherwise subject to governmental control. In practice, formal regulations that require boards of directors or trustees to assume an independent and strong role in corporate decision making are taken with varying degrees of seriousness and interpreted in different ways by government regulatory bodies. In some cases, government may insist that boards be representative of various public constituencies, that no obvious family or business relationships exist between executives and trustees, and that board members maintain a significant role in shaping service policies as well as financial decisions. In other cases, boards are allowed to be subservient to executive wishes or confined to pro forma matters of ratifying budgets and personnel appointments.

A conscientious policy of enforcing the independent strength of boards of directors could effectively influence discretionary entrepreneurial behavior. As fiduciary agents, more effective boards could thwart self-aggrandizement; as agents with whom executives must share power, more effective boards would reduce the ability of the executives and program managers to avoid accountability in the use of resources; as independent sources of judgment, boards could put the brakes on overbuilding, assuming that their members' own objectives did not also run in this direction. (Board members of nonprofit agencies are often accused of memorializing themselves through agency projects, especially buildings and other physical facilities).

It is worth a slight degression to recall that presidents or other active board members are sometimes themselves involved in entrepreneurial roles, usually in concert with executives. In such cases, remaining board members would need to independently exert their influence to preserve the accountability property of shared decision making in the nonprofit agency.

Realistically, however, a governmental policy to enforce shared decision making can only hope to be moderately successful for two principal reasons. (1) No matter how heavily the policy is pushed, government normally cannot actually control the selection of board members, but can only help shape the criteria and procedures within which the entrepreneur-executive and current board members make their choices. (For some types of nonprofits, government officials serve directly as trustees. These nonprofits might be classified as public or semi public rather than private nonprofit agencies.) (2) Board members themselves tend to be part-time and also preselected for their commitment to the style and purposes of the agency and its leadership. People are reluctant to join boards of agencies with which they are, in principle, at odds. As a result, and with some exceptions, boards will tend not to effectively restrain entrepreneurial indiscretions in the area of program planning. However, they will usually want to be part of the decision-making process, to ensure fiscal integrity, and to control aggrandizement within the time and resources that they have available. Even here, however, the prospects are mixed. As Cornuelle says:

> boards of trustees or directors . . . presumably are ultimately responsible for the institutions they govern, for the integrity of the operation. They are stewards of the money and sweat that individual citizens put into the colleges, churches, and welfare agencies they choose to help. These trustees are supposed to set policy and police the managers. Management, presumably, either works well or gets fired. . . . [But] the idea that laymen really control independent organizations has too often turned into a myth. Boards usually just raise money and vote "Yes" on whatever the professional managers want to do.[27]

Enforcing mandates for cooperative activity among nonprofit service providers is a governmental option in industries such as health care or social services that feature government-sponsored planning agencies whose goals include the more efficient use of community resources and more equitable distribution of services. A pioneering example is the Hill-Burton program in health care. As described by Dunlop:

> the biggest contribution of the Hill-Burton program was the administrative idea it introduced of a broad organizational [systems] perspective specified by the rational organization of health care institutions—for example, nursing homes in relation to hospitals—on a community-wide basis. This was the planning idea and the beginning of comprehensive health planning and regulation of provider entry.[28]

Planning agencies can encourage interagency cooperation through various potential means, including sponsorship of planning meetings and discussions, preparation of planning documents and master plans, requirements for reporting operational activities and for cross-referring clients, control over the entry of new programs through the application of need and necessity criteria, and funding of joint projects that feature the cooperation of multiple participating organizations. In effect, the enforcement of community-wide mechanisms of interagency coordination subjects individual entrepreneurial discretion to the rigors of comprehensive planning and peer pressure in areas in which competitive-market or other external forces tend to be weak in restraining such discretion. Therefore, the vigorous pursuit of interagency cooperation and system planning can conceivably inhibit discretionary nonprofit entrepreneuring behavior. In particular, expansionary tendencies by player-type entrepreneurs in given agencies would presumably be restrained by reference to global-planning requirements and peer review.

Policy and Policing

Increasing the intensity with which the nonprofit constraints are policed is not of as much interest in isolation as it is in conjunction with the formulation of other public policies, specifically those considered earlier in this chapter. In particular, it is worth asking whether some of the adverse effects (losses in trustworthiness) induced by such policies might be mitigated through an intensified policing effort, so that combinations of policy and policing achieve more effective social performance than is achieved by either alone. The answer to this question is a qualified yes in those circumstances where the policy option creates unique opportunities within the nonprofit sector of an industry. In such cases the policing mechanism may be useful as a complement to suppress dysfunctional behavior without simply shifting activity to other sectors or otherwise seriously suppressing the desired performance benefits. This principle can be applied to the four policy prescriptions as follows.

1. Nonprofitization creates unique opportunities in the nonprofit sector simply by ruling out industrial activity elsewhere. In the short run, enforcement of the nonprofit constraints could help suppress the discretionary leanings of income seekers and power seekers brought into the nonprofit sector by nonprofitization. In the long run, however, such policing might induce future such entrepreneurs to screen themselves into other industries because of the reduced discretionary opportunities. This latter effect may be minimal in view of other, more fundamental industry attributes that influence the industry-level screening process. Thus only minor losses of income seekers or power seekers to the industry may be expected from policing, either in the short run or the long run, although the discretionary excesses of these entrepreneurs maybe curbed.

The remaining question is whether policing will significantly reduce the vigor with which income seekers and power seekers undertake venture activity. If it does, the industry's responsiveness would be inhibited. Because nonprofitization does not immediately alter the industry's resource base or opportunities for advancement or necessarily change these radically over the long term, income seekers and power seekers may be expected to continue to be active, perhaps working harder to find legitimate income and power-based rewards. In this case, increased policing may serve as a useful complement to a nonprofitization policy, helping control the excesses in discretionary behavior that such a policy would induce, without crippling side effects.

2. Resource targeting specific to nonprofits creates unique opportunities in that sector in a manner similar to the nonprofitization policy. Specifically, if entrepreneurs wish to exploit the targeted resources, they must operate in the nonprofit context. Thus increased policing of the nonprofit constraints can serve as a complement here as well, helping ameliorate the losses of trustworthiness in the industry and nonprofit sector induced by resource-targeting policy. Because the latter policy increases the net resources available to the nonprofit sector and its respective industry, long-term screening losses of income seekers and power seekers or a significant reduction in the energy with which these types of entrepreneurs pursue their ventures seem even a less likely side effect of policing here than under nonprofitization.

3. Entry control applied differentially to the nonprofit sector creates some new opportunities in that sector (for example, for power seekers) while it reduces other opportunities (for example, for independents). Concurrent policing of the nonprofit constraints may therefore aid in controlling the discretionary activity of power seekers—both those activated in the short run within the nonprofit sector and those attracted to it in the long run—thus helping ameliorate the losses of trustworthiness that accompany entry control. However, as indicated by the analysis earlier, the activation and screening effects relative to power seekers are likely to be weak and

hence easily deterred or reversed by policing initiatives. Thus any gains in trustworthiness achieved by coupling policing with entry control are likely to be matched by losses in responsiveness of the nonprofit sector.

4. Professionalization is a non-sector-specific policy that in itself creates no opportunities unique to the nonprofit sector, although some of the entrepreneurs drawn to the industry in the long run, as a result of this policy—believers and poets in the social industries, poets, professionals, and perhaps architects in the creative industries, and professionals in the technical-service fields—may prefer to locate in the nonprofit sector. In none of these cases, however, does the loss of trustworthiness pose a serious threat. Hence complementary policing of nonprofit agencies offers no special benefits toward increasing an industry's trustworthiness, but it might inhibit the responsiveness of nonprofits by interfering with initiatives of its entrepreneurs.

Summary

This chapter has analyzed some of the public-policy implications of the theory developed in previous chapters. The first step was to consider what the performance characteristics of nonprofit sectors would be, if dominated in turn by each of the entrepreneurial stereotypes. Subsequently, the performance implications of various public policies were derived by determining how each policy would affect the screening and control of these various entrepreneurs within a nonprofit sector and industry.

Four social-performance criteria were established for service-producing sectors—trustworthiness, efficiency, responsiveness, and innovation. The analysis of entrepreneurial motivations indicated probable trade-offs between trustworthy and responsive patterns of sector behavior, whatever policy options were adopted.

Four policy alternatives, or proposals, often encountered in debates over nonprofit utilization and governance were analyzed—nonprofitization, resource targeting, entry control, and professionalizaton. All were seen to induce both short-run and long-run behavioral effects. In addition, several of these policies were seen to vary in their ultimate performance implications when coupled with increased public enforcement of the fiscal and organizational constraints that apply to nonprofit agencies.

Perhaps most significantly, these public policies were seen to induce some potential performance effects contrary to the presumed expectations of policy designers. In particular, increasing the nonprofit character of an industry, for example through nonprofitization or by targeting external resources specifically to that sector, was seen to be less productive than expected because it threatens the integrity (trustworthiness) of the nonprofit sector itself and, in the case of resource targeting, the character of the industry as a whole. This conclusion derives largely from consideration of the screening phenomenon, which implies that in the long run policy changes tend to rechannel existing motivations rather than to eliminate those motives.

Notes

1. Bruce C. Vladeck, *Unloving Care: The Nursing Home Tragedy* (New York: Basic Books, 1980).

2. John G. Simon, quoted in "Should For-Profits Go Non-profit?" *The Philanthropy Monthly*, October 1980.

3. Vladeck, *Unloving Care.*

4. Richard C. Cornuelle, *Reclaiming the American Dream* (Westminster, Md.: Random House, 1965).

5. Burton D. Dunlop, *The Growth of Nursing Home Care* (Lexington Mass.: Lexington Books, D. C. Heath and Company 1979).

6. Vladeck, *Unloving Care.*

7. Vladeck, *Unloving Care.*

8. Dunlop, *Nursing Home Care.*

9. Vladeck, *Unloving Care.*

10. Ken Judge, "The Privatisation of Social Care: Some Lessons from the USA" (Discussion Paper 161, Personal Social Services Research Unit, University of Kent, June 1980).

11. Vladeck, *Unloving Care.*

12. George J. Schutzer, "Prevalence of Nonprofit Organizations in the Broadcast Media" (PONPO working paper 14, Institution for Social and Policy Studies, Yale University, March 1980).

13. John G. Simon, "Should For-Profits."

14. Henry B. Hansmann, "Why Are Nonprofit Organizations Exempted from Corporate Income Taxation?" (PONPO working paper 23, Institution for Social and Policy Studies, Yale University, October 1980).

15. Vladeck, *Unloving Care.*

16. Edward M. Gramlich and Patricia P. Koshel, *Educational Performance Contracting* (Washington, D.C.: Brookings Institution, 1975).

17. Walter M. McQuade, "Management Problems Enter the Picture at Art Museums," *Fortune*, July 1974.

18. Henry B. Hansmann, "The Role of Nonprofit Enterprise," *Yale Law Journal*, April 1980.

19. Robert C. Clark, "Does the Nonprofit Form Fit the Hospital Industry?" *Harvard Law Review*, May 1980.

20. Schutzer, "Nonprofit Organizations in the Broadcasting Industry."

21. Dick Netzer, *The Subsidized Muse* (Cambridge: Cambridge University Press, 1978).

22. Karl E. Meyer, *The Art Museum: Power, Money, Ethics* (New York: William Morrow and Co., 1979).

23. Dennis R. Young and Stephen J. Finch, *Foster Care and Nonprofit Agencies* (Lexington, Mass.: Lexington Books, D.C. Heath and Company, 1977).

24. Vladeck, *Unloving Care*.

25. Ibid.

26. Bruce L.R. Smith, *The Rand Corporation* (Cambridge: Harvard University Press, 1966).

27. Cornuelle, *American Dream*.

28. Dunlop, *Nursing Home Care*.

11 Summary and Perspective

The most meaningful test of a descriptive social theory is not so much whether it is correct in all its details, but whether it stimulates people to think in some new and productive terms. These pages have put forth a theory that involves a series of descriptive details—most notably the specific motivations that characterize entrepreneurial behavior and the structural factors that influence the channeling and control of these motivations within different sectors of the economy. These descriptions are based on the author's empirical work and reading of the literature. Other observers may differ with the particulars presented here. Certainly the subject is open for further empirical study aimed at verifying and clarifying the nature of the parameters on which this analysis is based, but such refinement is secondary to the matter of attending to the essential ideas developed here. These ideas have implications for the way in which social scientists, particularly economists, model and analyze the behavior of nonprofit organizations as well as for the manner in which analysts and decision makers formulate and anticipate the consequences of policies designed to improve the performance or enlarge the role of nonprofits in the delivery of public services. For the social scientist, the principal lesson here is that the inherent diversity of participation in nonprofit organizations preordains failure in the search for any single, satisfactory, homogeneous model of a generic corporate nonprofit firm. Industry-wide perspectives that transcend sector boundaries are needed. For the policymaker, the essential point is that nonprofits cannot be properly viewed in isolation. Thus problems solved by ministering to nonprofits alone or by attempting to exploit the presumed purity of the nonprofit structure will tend only to change the shape or form of the problems rather than to make them disappear.

The central concept from which these lessons emanate is the mechanism of screening applied to entrepreneurial motivation, that is, the self-selection of entrepreneurial characters into industries and sectors that best suit their individual motives and styles. From this key notion, the following essential ideas have emerged:

1. The nonprofit sector is inherently flexible and diverse, capable of entertaining a wide variety of entrepreneurial motivations and giving such motivations substantial discretionary movement because of the absence of any dominant market or political-accountability mechanism.

2.   The behavior of a nonprofit sector cannot be represented by a single behavioral mode, but is best characterized as a mix of motivations, the nature of which depends on the relative attributes of the particular industry compared with other industries and on the relative structure of the nonprofit sector compared with other sectors that participate within the industry.

On the basis of attributes generally descriptive of nonprofit sectors relative to proprietary and public sectors, it has been argued that nonprofit sectors tend to exhibit mixes of entrepreneurial motivation that offer assurances of trustworthy behavior but a slowness of response to societal demands for service. This nominal nonprofit motivational mix may be expected to vary widely among industries, however.

3.   Screening of entrepreneurs is necessarily coarse because of the many factors involved in sector choice and the inertial tendencies (resistance to further screening) of entrepreneurs after early career decisions have been made. As a result, there will be discretionary behavior within nonprofit sectors, not only by those dominant types who have successfully screened themselves into sectors with attributes generally consistent with their motives, but also by those whose motives are relatively inconsistent with the structures within which they operate. The latter will tend to subvert the structural characteristics of their sectors, for example, the income-moderating constraints of nonprofits or the autonomy-reducing features of sectors that restrict new entry.

4.   The particular behavior patterns and social performance of a given service industry and its nonprofit component may be affected in a significant way by the implementation of various social-policy instruments that alter short-run behavior and long-run screening processes. These instruments include the nonprofitization of industries, the control of entry by new organizations, the requirement of professional certification of managerial and program personnel, and the targeting of public resources to the nonprofit parts of an industry.

5.   The expected effects of such public policies may not always match the good intentions of policymakers. For example, the screening and short-run behavior effects associated with such policies as nonprofitization and resource targeting may corrupt the nonprofit sector and subvert the intent of policymakers to make particular service industries more trustworthy.

6.   Complementarities may exist in the use of public resources to promote use of the nonprofit sector and to regulate that sector. For example, nonprofitization or the targeting of programmatic resources to nonprofit organizations might best be carried out in a regime of reinforced policing of the nondistribution and shared-decision-making mandates of organizations in that sector.

In short, the nonprofit sector must be viewed as an entity whose qualities can only be properly appreciated in the context of its economic environment. In particular, the performance qualities of this sector, inspired by its entrepreneurial elements, are seen to hinge on the screening and secondarily, on the restraint of these elements. The outcomes of these processes, in turn, depend on alternative opportunities outside the nonprofit sector as well as specific characteristics of organizations in the sector. Thus nonprofits must be seen as components of industrial systems, rather than as fully independent subsystems.

Much of the mystery surrounding nonprofits has emanated from an apparent lack of consistency in behavior and purpose of these organizations, both within and across industries. This lack of consistency has led to difficulty in describing these organizations, because there is no single, coherent, objective function with which to characterize the nonprofit agency. This difficulty is overcome by a screening theory that allows the nonprofit sector to filter out or absorb different behavioral elements as the ground rules for it and the other sectors with which it interfaces vary. In this light, the nonprofit sector has a residual character and is able to accommodate a range of entrepreneurial motivations that may clash with the more well-defined accountability and survival rules of the commercial and governmental sectors of the economy. The nonprofit sector can thus provide an invaluable, if changeable and fragile, refuge for enterprise and service provision based on various forms of idealism, emotional attachment, and intellectual purpose not accommodated elsewhere. The chemistry through which such motives mix with the more conventional economic and political drives commonly associated with other sectors is, however, also a crucial aspect of this analysis. This aspect fundamentally colors how well nonprofits can be expected to respond to demands for, and faithfully deliver, essential public services.

Index

About the Author

Dennis R. Young is professor and director of research in the W. Averell Harriman College for Urban and Policy Sciences of the State University of New York at Stony Brook. He is also a visiting faculty member of the Institution for Social and Policy Studies, Program on Non-Profit Organizations at Yale University. Dr. Young received the B.E. from the City College of New York, and the M.S. and the Ph.D. in engineering-economic systems from Stanford University. His principal research interests are the economic organization of public services and the behavior of nonprofit organizations. He is author of *How Shall We Collect the Garbage?: A Study in Economic Organization*, and coauthor of *Public Policy for Day Care of Young Children* and *Foster Care and Nonprofit Organizations*.